Aging
Wisely

AGING WISELY

Life from Fifty to Seventy-five Years

Viola B. Mecke, Ph.D., ABPP

Copyright © 2022 by Viola B. Mecke, Ph.D., ABPP.

Library of Congress Control Number:		2022916136
ISBN:	Hardcover	978-1-6698-4500-3
	Softcover	978-1-6698-4499-0
	eBook	978-1-6698-4498-3

All rights reserved. No part of this book may be reproduced or transmitted in any form or by any means, electronic or mechanical, including photocopying, recording, or by any information storage and retrieval system, without permission in writing from the copyright owner.

Any people depicted in stock imagery provided by Getty Images are models, and such images are being used for illustrative purposes only. Certain stock imagery © Getty Images.

Scripture quotations are from the Holy Bible, King James Version (Authorized Version). First published in 1611. Quoted from the KJV Classic Reference Bible, Copyright © 1983 by The Zondervan Corporation.

Print information available on the last page.

Rev. date: 09/21/2022

To order additional copies of this book, contact:
Xlibris
844-714-8691
www.Xlibris.com
Orders@Xlibris.com
843626

Contents

Preface vii
Acknowledgments ix
Introduction xi

PART I

Chapter 1   Life and Aging 1
Chapter 2   In the Beginning: The Initiation Losing Youth,
                Ages Fifty to Sixty-Five 7
Chapter 3   Retirement Years Not Young, Not Old: Ages Sixty-
                Five to Seventy-Five 15
Chapter 4   On the Bridge: The Age of Compassion Ages
                Seventy-Five to Eighty-Five 25
Chapter 5   The Curtain Call—The Encore Ages Eighty-Five Plus 35

PART II

Chapter 6   Our Challenge: Caring for Ourselves 51
Chapter 7   Are Our Emotions Growing Older? 53
Chapter 8   Capture Those Fears 65
Chapter 9   The Emotional Challenge of Loneliness 74
Chapter 10   Loves and Losses 81
Chapter 11   Loves and Losses, Part II: Homes and Possessions ... 89
Chapter 12   Resolving Those Problems Coping and Control 93
Chapter 13   Aging Wisely 104

Endnotes 107
References 111

Preface

Aging Wisely: Facing the Emotional Challenges from 50 to 85+ Years has emerged from my experiences of growing older. I have become increasingly convinced that feelings are the predominant force behind our actions, directing our choices and selecting our social relationships. My practice as a clinical psychologist centered on helping patients face those feelings that bind them from happiness in their lives.

Hidden feelings are often expressed in unknown and unbidden ways. For instance, I was especially impressed with one patient who avidly repeated that he had no feelings. His wife agreed. Nevertheless, during one session, he blinked while discussing a problem. When I questioned what he had felt at that moment, with effort, he said that he was afraid of what he had said, giving the key to recognizing his feelings. It is now recognized that as we grow older, we rely more on our feelings for the decisions and choices that we make.

"To your own self, be true" rings the bells of our hearts. To be true to ourselves is to be true to our feelings. Observing myself, family, friends, and patients as we have grown older instigated the thought that it might be easier if aging people were more aware that their feelings, their stresses, and their concerns about life were shared by others.

The growth of the field of developmental psychology now includes the phases of aging, as in other stages of growth. The research has familiarized us with the stresses that come at the time of life when we expected life would become easier, more content, and less fearful. Instead, we often find an increase in stress and anxiety alongside more pleasurable feelings of well-being.

Satisfaction with life calls for an emotional balance that brings contentment and quietude, and nurtures secure feelings. It requires accepting our positive strengths and our personal limitations to come to terms with ourselves. Hopefully, these thoughts will help the reader find that emotional balance, which ensures contentment and gratitude for life itself.

The illustrations that I have used in this book are partly from my own experiences as I have grown older. Names of all others have been fictionalized to conceal their identities. While my family members may recognize themselves, I have their permission to tell some of their stories.

In those moments when you are alone with your thoughts and memories, does quiet contentment seep through your being? Have you a sense of satisfaction and gratitude in your life? Here are some ideas. It is my hope this book will open pathways for greater pleasure and quietude in this last path of life.

Acknowledgments

Writing this book has been a challenge and a pleasure for me. Many have persuaded and encouraged me. Relatives, friends, and colleagues have supported my efforts. I thank them for their confidence that these words may prove helpful to others who are growing older. I am so grateful for the following:

Kerry Methner, editor of *Casa* magazine, whose untiring efforts in teaching the art of writing, reading the manuscript, and challenging ideas brought this book to fruition.

For the constant, valuable suggestions and encouragement of my brother, William Bloom, who read the first rough drafts of the book, without losing faith in my efforts.

Anita Mills was a loyal friend who read each draft, helping and reading throughout each stage of development of the book.

Alyce Dunn (my sister), Joanne Talbot, Ruth Levine, Mary Ann Norfleet, Paula Kunst, Maxine Underwood, and many others whose suggestions, stories, and encouragement were invaluable.

Finally, many thanks and much gratitude to Mary Flores and Josh Prince of the Xlibris Publishing Company who tolerated my idiosyncrasies and encouraged me throughout the process of publishing the book.

INTRODUCTION

Old age: balding, wrinkles, sore feet, saggy thighs, bifocals, senior discounts, slowed healing, cataracts, chicken skin, wills, sex after seventy, vertigo, no driving, managed care, hearing aids, canes, memory loss, walkers, wheelchairs, bruises, incontinence, broken hips, bruised egos, and so on.

What is it like to grow old, then older? This book will soften myths attributed to older senior citizens, demonstrate their strengths, and enlighten their pathways. The cultural norms have not provided many pleasant expectations or hope for these last years. *Aging Wisely* and its sequel, *The Ups and Downs of Growing Older*, show that in contrast to popular myths, aging brings a deeper enjoyment and pleasure to life. Both professional and practical approaches to the topics are discussed in this little book. The physical changes do not spoil the spirit of enjoyment and pleasure that is unique in aging. Growing older brings new gratifications, satisfactions, and expectations, often in contradiction to the current social ideas.

Present culture holds expectations of aging that are often untrue or hold a grain of truth that misrepresents the truth. These expectations are *myths*—ideas that are widely held beliefs but false. Look at some of these myths:[1]

> Myth 1: Aging means the end of cognitive development and new learning. The evidence suggests that learning new material is possible and is often accomplished.
>
> Myth 2: When you get older, you will inevitably experience dementia or another memory disorder. The

research suggests brain stimulation through new activities can help the brain to remain active and learn new material.

Myth 3: Depression is normal in older adults; isolation and aloneness incite depression as a person ages. The research is contrary, for older adults are less likely to become depressed than younger adults.

Myth 4: Older persons should avoid strenuous exercising to avoid injury. A misrepresentation. On the contrary, there is much to gain by being physically active and much to lose by sitting too much.

Myth 5: Older persons do not need as much sleep as when younger. Not true: older persons still require seven to nine hours of sleep per night. Following a regular sleep pattern without afternoon naps and avoiding the light emitted from electronics may help a person receive the rest that is needed for health.

Other myths are also frequently verbalized, such as being too old to change habits, such as quitting smoking; older women will suffer with osteoporosis; seniors are unhappy; seniors are not productive; seniors cannot be creative; and seniors are cranky.

We shall see that these general statements describing older persons do not define aging and contain many assumptions that increase a negative attitude toward growing older and being older. And while each or all may pertain to individuals, they do not present the actuality of being or becoming older.

The myths give rise to and support the current discriminatory attitudes against older people. Negative expectations of aging have been with us for many centuries. Discriminatory feelings are not new. Long ago, the respect and esteem for the world of elders disappeared. For example, listen to the words of Macbeth, given to us by Shakespeare in the seventeenth century. Here are the words of Shakespeare from the play *Macbeth*.[2]

> I have lived long enough, my way of life
> Is fallen to the sere, the yellow leaf,
> And that which should accompany old age,
> As honor, love, obedience, troops of friends,
> I must not look to have, but in their stead,

Curses, not loud but deep, mouth-honor, breath
Which the poor heart would fain deny and dare not.

The negative attitudes noted by Macbeth continue in the present day. Discrimination prevails; the hope for honor, respect, and courtesy is not present in our culture. *Aging Wisely* presents the lives of senior citizens with the activity, strength, and feelings that dominate their lives.

Read on, dear reader, and enjoy the picture of senior citizens solving the difficulties that are met, to age wisely.

Part I

Chapter 1

Life and Aging

Life can only be understood backwards, but it must be lived forwards.
—Soren Kierkegaard

Aging wisely seems an impossibility, a dream, as if knowing how to age might erase the aging itself. Rather, it means using experience as a guide, anticipating what happens to us as we grow older, selecting choices that enrich who we are, and having a means of approaching and solving problems that will provide the best living possible as we grow old.

I Know More Now Than I Used To

Or so it would seem. I am eighty-five years old and would like to put some of my experiences in perspective. If I can understand my past, perhaps I can help other people meet the emotional complexities of aging and understand that their concerns and anxieties are normal. And they can be prepared to meet them. Contentment and joy come from within. It is never too late to find that inner space that opens to contentment and enjoyment in life.

Throughout my life, I have been fascinated by people and how they respond to situations. Some people express their feelings so easily, and others seem to have no emotional reactions. Growing up in a family of seven children, I remember trying to anticipate how each of my sisters and brothers and both of my parents would feel and react to situations that were coming. So I became a psychologist.

For this book, I will focus on the emotional challenges that one meets in later life. Many people fantasize that, in age, the problems of life have been resolved. After all, responsibilities have let up, and professional and work responsibilities disappear. Yet, with age, sometimes the opposite is true.

Emotional demands are often heightened, difficult choices must be made, and illness is almost universal. Worse, it often seems that most of the emotional reserves we've spent our lives developing are suddenly used up. Now challenges demand even more from our being, our health, and our mental strength.

Sorrow comes our way. It is a deep sadness and distress at the loss of someone. And yes, I have known sorrow. Sorrows that linger are the loss of my mother and oldest sister. These are the people whose presence is with me every day, reminding me of the importance of living well and especially being attuned to others.

The love from my mother lives in me. She had a devotion to her children that gave them the basis for a life of happiness. I also remember the guidance of my sister: "Beyond a wholesome discipline, be gentle with yourself" and "Keep peace with your soul, in all that you do."

Each sorrow affects us, often in different ways. There is a peace that can be found through sorrow—the knowledge that love stays with you. We will take a deeper look at sorrow, its implications for living and loving, and how to let it enrich our life.

Loneliness may descend. Loneliness descends upon many an older person. It is a terrible, awful plight. It is a sense of desperation, of lost contact with others and oneself. It is a painful distress.

I was lonely after my husband died. In the next two years, I moved from my home of thirty years, leaving many friends, neighbors, and colleagues. They were times of feeling lost and alone. I spent time walking by the ocean; and, the rhythm of the waves was calming. It was that open space, watching the waves roll onto the shore, the rhythm of life healed. Solitude refreshed my spirit.

Loneliness is the time to take charge of one's life and feelings. More than one half of people over seventy say they are lonely and have no meaningful, close contact with others. In contrast, aloneness is often a welcomed quiet, good for the soul and refreshing to the spirit. Loneliness searches for meaningfulness and a balm for the bruise of loss.

Love remains with us—love, a magical word. The importance of bonds with others deepens as we age. The warmth of comfort, safety, and joy in the presence of those we love provides an eloquence for life. Losses of those who have endowed us with care and love have a profound impact on our feelings, health, and life itself. Love has supplied nurturance for the soul; it is not taken away in illness or death.

Loves and losses are of utmost importance in the aging process. While love becomes increasingly more appreciated, losing those with whom we are closely bonded becomes critical. The grief that follows can be assuaged by more love.

Joy resides within. There is a core of exuberance. Joy and happiness are not owned by youth. They are more fully experienced as we grow older. Surely in this last phase of living, there may be physical problems to manage. We may have lost partners, relatives, and friends through death. Yet joy and happiness can remain.

The past is there and sometimes wants attention in memories. Choices that were disappointing were made. Even so, the spirit can be free to rejoice in life itself—the past, the present, and the morrow. Although aging brings emotional challenges, growing older can become a time for knowing the fullness of the spirit.

Physical distress is not unusual. Feelings that come with the normal physical changes of aging bring a change in our self-concept, even when we try to deny them. Now we enter a period of continuous physical changes.

Illness or disability come gradually or besiege us, like a drowning cascade. And illness demands our attention, affects our mood, and challenges us to maintain a good feeling about life. Physical problems are something to anticipate and not deny. This will show the path for coping with whatever befalls us.

And there are other feelings that come our way, with the new and surprising challenges that aging may bring. Fears come. As we encounter each new situation, such as losing independence or losing control over situations, fearfulness and anxieties arise. We shall investigate the source and resolution of these feelings in the last half of the book.

I Know More about Time

I know that time is constant and that each day and year passes with the same real speed. It did not always seem that way. Some days and years moved too quickly; others dragged by, seemingly endless. As a child, when good events were anticipated, time seemed too long. Santa Claus would never come; making the potato salad for a picnic took too long; I would never be old enough to drive a car; and I might never meet the man of my dreams. Santa came; the picnic was fun; I drove; and I married. Now, time lags or speeds by. Time's speed is a counterpart of moods and feelings.

The internal sense of time varies with the emotional tone of events—times of happiness fly by, and times of sadness and loneliness drag by endlessly. Time and feelings blend. They define the moments of life.

Now in my eighties, as I look back, I recognize instances of time that marked significant changes in my life. There are phases in growing older that mark changes for me and, I think, for all.

The *phase of fulfillment* is the first phase of aging. The "middle ages" began when a younger female colleague held a door open for me. I looked at her in amazement! Why would she do that? In an instant, it dawned on me. I was an older woman, of course!

Time speeds by during the years of fifty to sixty-five. I was a busy professional, merging clinical and academic work. Life could not slow down to give more time for work or fun. Weekends sped by too quickly. It was a time of fulfillment of my life's work, pleasure with friends, and contentment with my family.

For many, these are busy and often stressful years. Problems typical to this age, such as family changes, work stresses, and the search for personal meaning share importance.

The *phase of retirement* (ages sixty-five to seventy-five) marks a pulling back from work. It brings a critical change in life. For some, it is easy and welcome; it was free from demands and expectations; for others, it is distressful and undesired, a loss of identity. For me, retirement brought a cascade of difficult emotional challenges. One situation after another tumbled upon me, without respite.

The years began with the death of my husband, then my bout with cancer, death of my sister-in-law, and heart surgery of my brother. In retrospect, they were awful years. Living through them was a normal course in life. They were challenges to be managed. Even so, retirement was time for me and time for family.

The *productive phase* (from seventy-five to eighty-five years) is a time of acknowledging that we are in the class of older citizens, yet we may not feel old. We acknowledge the limited time of life. It brings a need for nearness to family and friends and compassion for others. It is also a time to fulfill dreams of a lifetime—travel, new activities, creative ventures.

It is a period for reconstruction of life's activities, including finding new friends, increasing social participation, entering volunteer activities, adjusting to being older with less energy, and recognizing some physical limitations. For most of us, it is a time of reflection and a clarification of patterns that have characterized one's life. It often uses reminiscence as a tool for recovering significant events of life.

The *phase of loving living* (ages eighty-five and on) is the path of completing the cycle of life. For some, it is filled with sorrow and illness. For others, it is a gift and opportunity to fulfill a longing of the heart.

For me, this phase of life has been wonderful. Oh yes, I am older; I move with less agility and rhythm, and I have some physical ailments. But inner freedom has come. It is as if the dawn has burst into my soul. A love for all enveloped me, even for two little wrens sitting closely together, quietly, on the patio.

It was an inner euphoria. Poems rolled from that inner space—poems of joy and life. They reached for understanding the times, events, and feelings of life.

I know that time here is limited. I do not know what follows death, only that I want to be peacefully and contentedly ready. If I have helped one person manage the stresses, tribulations, and anxieties of aging with this writing, my desire is fulfilled. I sincerely hope these following pages will be helpful to you and enrich the journey of life as you also age.

I Know There Is Much More to Know

To know oneself is to know the feelings that reside in that inner space. To know oneself is to find a comfort and a resilience that accepts the variances in situations and a more complete acceptance of others. It is the key to living and to aging wisely.

I will discuss the phases of aging, using both my personal experience and professional knowledge to guide the way. I hope to show how to greet the emotional stresses that aging brings so that it can become a time for realizing the fullness of life. Hopefully, the book will be an aid to bring about better resolutions of problems and help us all to age more wisely.

Chapter 2

In the Beginning: The Initiation Losing Youth, Ages Fifty to Sixty-Five

Time is here. The time we have been waiting for. Time has brought us to the acme of our life. Responsibilities are lessening. Time for the empty nest. The time of competence and confidence. A new time.

Reaching the age of fifty, we are in the beginning period of the loss of youthfulness. We are mature and maturing. These are often lively and good years. We have developed a sense of ourselves, feelings of self-confidence, and a sense of competence about what we do well. Children are either adolescents or have left home to live on their own. Grandchildren may be there, marking the third generation. Friendships and social activities flourish and play an important role in daily life. These years represent the peak of performance at work. With the responsibilities of life lessening, we are looking forward to time for ourselves, to fulfill some dreams and develop new activities.

At a time when it seems the difficult problems are coming to an end, new challenges arise. Stress comes. This generation, the baby boomers born between 1946 and 1964, presently make up 20 percent of the American population. They have enjoyed some good economic times. You now encounter new stresses. Physical changes bring conscious awareness of growing older. There are changes taking place within the family, such as children leave home, marital relationships are often reevaluated, friendships become richer or fade away, and stresses in the workplace occur as younger people replace experienced workers.

The relationship with your spouse may be affected. Aging parents may become a new responsibility, and you find yourself caught between responsibilities for children and parents. Reentry into the work world, possible career transitions, declining career opportunities, and preparations for retirement linger in the atmosphere as stressful adjustments.

Tension in any home has emotional repercussions, and much depends on the resolutions. Frustration, anger, tenseness, and so forth can result in anxiety, sadness, or laughter. Resolution strengthens family bonds.

The emotional challenges are (1) reactions to physical changes that mark the loss of youthfulness, (2) coming to terms with an empty nest, and (3) changing family relationships.

Emotional Reactions to Middle Age

Physical changes take place for both men and women during this period. While health, as well as age, marks the passage from one phase to another, normal physical changes mark the beginning of this phase. Menopause for women and andropause for men force attention to the natural changes of the body. These changes compel a realization of being mature, of no longer being "young," and elicit fear of growing old.

The fears provoked by the idea of becoming older are often covered by drastic steps taken to maintain a youthful appearance, to deny the signs of aging, and keep an appearance of youthfulness, if possible. Our present culture places an emphasis on youthfulness and remaining youthful. Advertisements, literature, and pharmaceutical messages focus on ways to avoid or delay the natural changes that come with age. Both men and women spend hours in the gym, in Pilates or tai chi classes, running or bicycling, and other activities to stay strong and slim and to keep muscular strength. These activities compensate for a passive, inactive, sitting culture.

Women may become emotionally reactive and sensitive during menopause. Menopause is an undeniable sign of getting older and brings with it a tendency to add weight as the body becomes rounder. Even fifty years ago, my mother expressed concern about her moderate weight gain during this time, to which my father would reply, "It gives me more to love." She never was obese.

Nearly 95 percent of women are bothered by mood swings during the menopausal period. Hormonal changes bring on a bevy of temporary emotional reactions, such as unnerving mood swings that can vary from a high to moods of depression. Some moods are energy loaded, and some show delight in unimportant events, such as the beautiful weather, or loving everyone, or a buying spree. At an extreme, it is a wild roller-coaster ride of emotions, such as bouts of crying, sorrow, despair, anger, anxieties, or fear. Dramatic as they may be, mood swings pass quickly, leaving some confusion about the variations from normal mood.[i]

Women become increasingly concerned about the loss of attractiveness, the loss of appeal to their husbands, and the appearance of aging, even to other women. The stress of growing older, of *looking* older, takes its toll. For in their anxiety, they try to deny—to the world and themselves—its effects. Women turn to efforts such as facial lifts, hair coloring, makeup, faddish dressing style, or Botox. And believe me, I am not making negative value statements, for I have done some of them. Spending hours having my blond-turning-dark hair getting streaked in a salon makes me now wonder why. I simply recognize the common anxiety brought on by fears of not being as attractive and the efforts to alleviate it. The fears are subtle, often unconscious—but they push us to try to control the events.

Men have their concerns too—although they often hide them. Men fear baldness, gray hair, losing muscular strength, or lessening of sexual prowess. They too have physical changes brought by a decrease in hormones, the experience of *andropause*, the male equivalent of menopause.[ii] The middle-aged stomach, the roving eye, the lazy syndrome, irritability, and depression are signals—although often ignored under a guise of a male prerogative.[iii]

Relationships between spouses may meet a bump in the road at this time because both face fears of becoming older. When a good partnership has developed, each other's changes, moods, and idiosyncrasies are accepted. When the anxieties become greater, emotion-laded reactions may mar the partnership with unanticipated irritability and life dissatisfaction. Fran and Tony are such a couple. For example, Fran, a very gracious person of fifty-two years, had always taken pride in her appearance, but in the last four or five years, she gained ten pounds. When their son made a disparaging comment about her weight gain, she became very self-conscious. Fran then repeatedly sought reassurance from Tony, her husband, that she was still attractive, that he still loved her. Tony, ten years older, was at the same time trying Viagra, not wanting to admit some loss of sexual drive. Although he had added over ten pounds at the same time, his weight drew no negative comments. Both Fran and Tony were hanging on to as much youth as possible.

The envy of the beauty of youth may be intense. Thomas Mann describes these attractions in the novel *Death in Venice*. His hero of fifty years takes a last trip to Venice, where he falls in love with a teenage boy. Mann writes, "This was very frenzy—and without a scruple ... Mind and heart were drunk with passion ... The envy of an older man scrutinizing the beauty of youth."

Emotional Renewal of the Partnership

For twenty or more years, children, work responsibilities, finances, and miscellaneous problems have claimed the attention of the marriage. Now you two are alone; the children move, whether to college or to their own home.

Some parents have looked forward eagerly to children growing up, attending college, or settling down with their own families. They are pleased with each step the child takes toward independence and life. Yet their absence brings a sense of sadness—and an eagerness to hear from them, if not daily, often. "What do we talk about now, without the children here?" The house seems empty, even desolate without them.

Others are overly eager to have the house for themselves, to be alone without the responsibilities of children. One mother I knew was definite about this. She said, "I have always told them, 'When you are eighteen, you are out of my house!'" And she meant it too. In an atmosphere like this, the child may be just as eager to turn eighteen!

For mothers whose main responsibility has been parenting, it may be a period of grief and some depression. For the stay-at-home parent (this includes about 15 percent of fathers), it is a crucial time. Decisions will be made that will affect the balance in the spousal relationship. It is a new period that will bring emotional renewal to the home scene—whether to return to school, spend time with favorite activities, or resume their work life. Some parents enjoy grandparenting! Others say, "I will never be a babysitter." For both, it is a time that brings a renewed evaluation of life.

The empty nest may be challenging for couples whose marriage has revolved around their children and family. Their discussions and communication have centered on the children. For these couples, the loss may be greater, and the emotional closeness that parenting brought leaves a void. What shall they talk about? What shall they do? The good part is the sadness caused by the empty nest may be relieved through the opportunity to rekindle the pleasure, intimacy, and meaning of the parents' relationship. It becomes a time to renew love—time for a new honeymoon, time to alleviate the anxieties provoked by this new togetherness.

Here you are, as it was when you began life together. The emotional challenge for both revolves around the question of "Who am I?" without being a parent. The focus turns to each other—talking together, planning activities alone or together, pleasing each other. Recovering your early relationship and devotion may take conscious effort. It is a time for reflection on the future and planning to fulfill the goals and interests that have been ignored.

Changes in Family Relationships

These are good years to enjoy your family. Children are older; they are fun to be with. You appreciate that parental responsibilities have been alleviated. As children grew older, your role gradually changed from protection, guidance, and responsibility to that of suggestions and support. In family interactions, mutual respect and dignity have come. Parents are free from a protective role; the adolescent or adult child develops opinions of his/her own, sometimes in contradiction to parents but more often following the patterns the parents have set. Holidays with children provide enjoyment and continuity.

Adult children may ask for guidance from parents and then may proceed on a different path, one they choose. This may bring tension between the parents and adult children. Rather, parents learn to watch, suggest, and worry but not command.

In one study, baby boomers were asked for a daily report about the stresses or tension that occurred in their home over a period of eight consecutive days. They reported that incidents of stress or tension were present on half of the days, with the tense period lasting up to two hours. Most of the tension (60 percent) involved another person: for instance, a husband and wife arguing about finances, arguments about teenagers' use of the car, or dissension at work. The results indicated the higher the level of education and income, the fewer the stresses reported in the home

(Whitbourne and Willis 2006). It seemed that more coping skills were available to these parents.

Emotional stress results in anger or depression, fears, or sadness. When it becomes a problem with unsatisfactory results or the problem remains unresolved, friction may linger and spoil the cohesiveness of a relationship. Professional counseling may be helpful.

Grandchildren bring an awareness of the continuity of life. This sense of generational continuity stimulates a powerful drive to know more about the family background. For instance, Alex Haley, author of *Roots*, pursued stories told him by his grandmother to track his maternal family back to a youth in the Gambia who had been kidnapped and brought to the United States as a slave.[v] He writes, "I was delighted to discover that my great-grandfather was a musician who played the violin. As a child, I had yearned to have violin lessons." Uncovering family origins and lore is an exciting and interesting way to bring the past to the present—and to understand family patterns that continue throughout generations.

One source of stress in the family comes with the aging, illness, or disabilities of the grandparents. Often enough, grandparents may rely on their children for help, even though they do not wish to place responsibilities on the children. The problem of managing a home, caring for children and/or grandchildren, caring for aging parents, responding positively and supportively to the spouse, and needing time for themselves presents emotional strains on the couple. Parents are caught in between the responsibilities and the emotional demands on their time and energy; these responsibilities come just when they were looking forward to time for themselves. These problems bring intense stress—and in turn can have negative emotional or health effects on the caring persons.

The Search for Clarity

Generally, high levels of well-being persist during this time. It is a time of self-confidence and of feelings of competence. People now possess personal skills and resources that experience and maturity have brought. There is a sense of confidence in the working life, even if changing course. The emotional challenges focus on taking pleasure and enjoyment from life and responding to the sadness or fears that come. Surely, life passes through stormy times; it is meeting them with acceptance and responding to them with resilience that provides the grace not available in earlier years.

This phase of life is an excellent time to take a picture of the inner self. How can you sharpen the image of yourself—so that who you are becomes closer to the person you want to be? How can you improve the emotional quality of your relationship with your mate? Your family? Making new goals during this phase of life often brings a renewal of the zest for life that brings enjoyment in the time to come.

Robert Frost wrote:

> The woods are lovely, dark, and deep,
> But I have promises to keep,
> And miles to go before I sleep.

In this phase of life, there is much living yet to do, with changes in roles and expectations, different and new feelings to come, and different perspectives to have for yourself and your life.

The emotional challenges of this period of life involve the following:

Knowing yourself, as Socrates recommended. Take time to recognize your feelings and their source. Then think before reacting, for feelings do not always deserve expression. Relax with physical and situational changes; accept them with humor and difficult days with grace. Meet the sad mood and depressing days with a smile for another person, or sing a song, or take a walk.

For your partner: accept his/her moods, feelings, and actions; become curious about preferences, wishes, or dreams for the present and future; tell and show your love—often.

For children: Pull back graciously from control over your children-becoming-adults. Provide support when asked by helping them think through their own problems and encourage their choices. Let yourself know you cannot protect them from all problems that life may present. Give up the need to control and the urge to discipline.

For your parents: Anticipate the present and future needs they may have by talking and planning with them. Discuss the support they may want and the options they might have.

Remain active and encouraging with friends; engage regularly with your social groups.

Time, like air, is the spirit of life. It is fragile yet not touchable. Time can drag us down into the depths of our souls. It can lie heavily upon our shoulders. Time is sometimes fragrant with the sweetness of a flower. It can float with the lightness of a breeze. It is ethereal yet real. It is ours.

CHAPTER 3

Retirement Years
Not Young, Not Old: Ages Sixty-Five to Seventy-Five

The time has come. In the retirement phase of life, we enter a borderland—not young, not old. We are stepping down from the mainstream and entering a quieter time of life. Our life experience has prepared us for this. In this borderland, life resounds with contentment. We can take the opportunity to contemplate the gifts we have to offer our family, friends, and community.

It is no longer the first wrinkle and gray hair greeting us in the mirror every day. Oh, another one! I never saw that one before ... a frown ... a surge of sadness. We do not like those reminders that we are changing, that we are growing older. Aging happens ... unbidden.

It's a good time and a good age. Yet these are the years that bring a realization that we are in the older class of citizens—the *young old* class. The years have brought many changes. While many now work no longer, others are choosing to continue work, and some are enjoying part-time work in a different field. So it is time to enjoy life, to do those things we have put off. Now is the opportunity to fulfill long-postponed wishes and dreams.

It is a time when intimacy, trust, and love with a spouse may be deepened as more activities are enjoyed together. There is a new challenge of growing old together. What time will be together? What time to have for my own activity? Many have good health to enjoy this new age. Others, sadly, have already begun to experience illnesses and/or disabilities.

"I am happier now than I have ever been," reported a friend who was visiting while attending her granddaughter's college graduation. It was wonderful to hear these words, for she had faced many challenges, including health and family difficulties. At the age of seventy-six, she was comfortable with her life. Her spirits were lively and her happiness obvious.

There are many reasons for retirement. Some retire because they want to engage in another life plan; some retire because of the loss of physical vigor or other health reasons; and most because employers expect it. When retirement is voluntary, the primary reasons given are "more time with my family" or "I want to do other things." In the two years following retirement, 61 percent are very satisfied without the daily demands of work. One-third are moderately content. For a few (7 percent), the loss of work is devastating. And sadly, for those who retire at age sixty-five, there is an "elevation in death rates during the third and fourth years after retirement" (Spector 2006).

The year of retirement is one of the transitions in lifestyle, activities, relationships, and especially feelings. The transitions from scheduled time to unscheduled activities become days of freedom or an anxiety-ridden search for something to do. It is a transition from controlled activities at work to doing whatever you want. Relationships change, becoming closer and warmer or exacerbating differences with family and friends. Feelings in transition—sadness and nostalgia, exuberance and depression, contentment and anxiety, anticipation and disappointment—all may be there. These feelings mark the behavior during the transition to retirement.

Emotional reactions to retirement fall into three classes: (1) freedom and relief, (2) acceptance, and (3) sadness and health problems.

Freedom and Relief

For many, retirement brings a release from the demands of earning a living, from the control of others, from meeting expectations, or from a heartily disliked working situation. An example of transition: One colleague, Patricia, retired after twenty-five years of working in an exhausting and stressful position, in which she dealt with crises daily. She felt unusually liberated when she retired. She moved away from a smog-ridden city to a small town. Involved in handicrafts, she found like-minded people and devoted her time to painting, wood carving, and glass decorations. Her talents were financially rewarding. Then she wanted to see the country, so she purchased a motor home. For two years, she traveled from one coast to the other. And now, at seventy-two, she is fulfilling yet another life dream. Ever since her grandfather had placed her on a horse when she was four years old, she had wanted a horse. She purchased a well-trained fourteen-year-old horse, took riding lessons, and enjoys her rides along the coast or in the forest. Her retirement years have been fulfilling and gratifying, despite a few health problems.

Patricia was exuberant with retirement, elated, and energetic. She had made plans. Hopefully, you are planning what you want to do after work life. There are new and older interests to pursue—gardening, writing, painting, or reading. Or now is the time to travel, explore the world, or visit family that lives afar.

It is your opportunity to try out new ideas, new ventures. One retired attorney did just that. Curious about some common products in life, he first made beer in his basement—it did not turn out well. He then tried making soap. That worked better, and he gave special handmade soap to friends. This "young old" age can be an exciting, fulfilling time.

The most important factor is you, yourself, as a person. You will profit from personality qualities, such as curiosity about every day, an ability to accept changes, a good sense of humor, and a love of life; these qualities ease a stressful period.

Acceptance

It is important that we accept that retirement is here, now—at age sixty-five, perhaps as an employment policy of the company. Perhaps there have been no plans made, no ideas of what to do with all that time. Perhaps there are fears associated with it—not just that there will be nothing to do, but financial constraints may not be secure. Socioeconomic status is a major factor that may determine satisfaction after retirement. For the middle and upper classes, financial restraints are often not severe. And that helps much. For the working-class members who have not been able to save or do not receive a pension from employers, the financial strain is significant. It is estimated that 47 percent of retirees over sixty-five years old would fall into the poverty level without the income provided by Social Security. And importantly, it is reported that social class not only affects health but also speeds up the aging process itself. It has been shown that people in lower economic and working social classes are even biologically older than those in higher social classes—because of a lack of good nutrition, less education, less satisfactory living conditions, stress, and insufficient health services (Spector 2006).

Nevertheless, retirement is the next step in life. For instance, Susan, a mother of three adult children, has just turned sixty-five. Her husband has not worked regularly for ten years, so she has been the breadwinner; she worked as a housekeeper for others. She is a tall, imposing person with a positive, pleasant outlook. She is confident that all will go well enough for them. Nothing seems to faze her. She is energetic and healthy, feels in control of her life, and is happy with her family. She has learned the hard way that she no longer controls her children's lives or their families. Sometimes she has even risked losing the relationship because of her *suggestions* for the grandchildren. She is delighted to have Medicare for future medical expenses. Pragmatic to the hilt, when asked how it feels to be getting older, she responds, "I'll take whatever comes." She has a resilience that will be with her for whatever transitions come.

The transitions into retirement are managed with the same spirit that has guided our lives. The loss of work as a daily activity, the loss of social relationships with those with whom we have worked—sometimes for years of work-related friendships—and even of supervisors or managers whose encouragement was provided - will bring sadness. Spirits sag, and moods may be depressed in the early days of retirement. A rule of thumb is that it takes about a year to establish a new pattern for the day's activities. The same zest for life, interest in the world about us, and relationships with family and friends come to aid in easing the adjustment to a new pattern of life. Primary factors that determine the reaction to retirement will be maintaining friendly, supportive relationships, having a positive outlook, and your health status.

Dissatisfaction and Dread

For some, their existence and life have been defined by work. The loss of the work role may bring a temporary depression, which usually disappears as other activities fill the void. When doing nothing and being no one brings an attitude of meaninglessness of life, a sense of emptiness, even despair, takes over. These are unfortunate persons, and they soon develop increasing health problems. They become anxious and morose and chase away any sense of being wanted or loved. Pulling into themselves, focusing on misery, they give little to others. Nothing satisfies. There is no gratification. Depression settles in when hope and the love of life disappear.

Changing Relationships with Spouse and Family

The relationship between couples may undergo subtle and not-so-subtle changes as more time and activities are spent together after retirement. Daily duties may become areas of cooperation or dispute. For instance, do you arise together? Eat all meals together? Who does the cooking? Will you alternate roles? Do you do everything together? Do you have interests to pursue together? Do you have individual interests or activities? Who plans for the day or week or travel or visits?

The first question is whether you are satisfied with retirement or with the retirement of your spouse. One adage stated, "When a man retires, his wife gets twice the husband and half the salary."[vi] This illustrates the reaction before it was common for both partners to be working. Now that it is more usual for both to work, the patterns are more complex. The following has been found:

- 77 percent of retirees express satisfaction with retirement.
- Only 67 percent of their spouses are satisfied.
- Husbands of wives who retire are more satisfied than wives of retired husbands.
- Couples made up of retired wives and *nonmanagerial* husbands are eight times more likely to report that both are satisfied with retirement than when the husband was in a managerial role.
- Couples are more satisfied with retirement when the wife retires from a *managerial* or *professional* job. (Smith and Moen 2004)

These statistics suggest that, even currently, upon retirement, there is a pullback to the cultural expectations that women belong at home, while husbands do not. They also suggest that men may fear their wives will maintain dominance at home. In the present day, as both have been working, hopefully the couple may be more prepared for a partnership in retirement.

The emotional challenges both face are intertwined with the stress of adjusting to a new life pattern, which often enough may seem out of control. Reports from men who have retired include the following:

- I traveled a lot in my job; when I retired, I felt like a visitor, an outsider person in my own house.
- My wife told me that she could not tolerate having me at home all the time. She said I had to get out of the house most of the day.
- It was like a dream. I did not know what to do. I just wandered around.
- I stayed in bed until I had to get up.

And wives reported the following:

- He is underfoot all day. No matter where I turn, he is there.
- Now I must prepare three meals every day. That is hardly retirement for me.
- I feel sorry for him; he has nothing to do.
- I have no time for myself; he is always there.
- I am not going to be the babysitter for my grandchildren.

Both men and women have adjustments to make. Small changes in the daily pattern of life may become sources of humor and enjoyment or provoke disgruntlement, anger, or depression. My parents settled their roles easily. Mother took care of the house; Dad had responsibility for the outside—gardening, lawn, garage, and so on. They had their own space. Yet as they grew older, roles changed, and they shared more mundane activities. For instance, my father would peel the potatoes while they prepared dinner together. Mother was more active and pulled the weeds in their small garden; Dad had back problems. Some of these changes come through the effects of aging but mostly through the melding of their personalities, wishes, and emotional closeness.

So, yes, retirement and aging bring changes in the relationship with a partner. It can be an opportunity to expand the relationship. As they spend more time with each other and do more activities together, they become aware of gestures or facial grimaces they did not recognize before. The relationship will deepen. It is a time for knowing each other better and for creating togetherness in experiences. To become aware of a partner's feelings that are different and unexpected is to know them better, to know each other in a more intimate way. The warmth of my husband's smile as he talked with a neighbor's son and other neighborhood children resides deep within me. His smile brought joy to my heart.

Increased intimacy brings warmth and closeness that knows, respects, and honors the individuality of the other. I have heard many a retired person say, "I learn something new about her or him every day."

Transitions in Self-Concept

Another emotional challenge that comes during this stage is acceptance of the new role of "not working." This requires a subtle and gradual change in the way we think of ourselves and our life. It may be a startling revolution, bringing new feelings. For example, I was a psychologist for forty years. No longer may I correctly say, "I am a psychologist." I am no longer teaching students or counseling people. Friends, knowing I had written a book, would introduce me as a writer. This disturbed me at first, for I did not *feel* like a writer. It was a strange identity, and I would deny it, saying, "Oh no, I am not." It does not disturb me anymore. It is what I am doing. As time passes, there is a realization that the techniques, information, or activities in our former work life have changed so much that our knowledge, once expertise, is now passé. We are no longer up to date.

Self-concept is how we think of ourselves. Sometimes the sense of self is work related, as in "I am a teacher." Other times, it refers to personality traits, such as "I am kind," "I am generous," or "I am grouchy." Or sometimes it refers to a social relationship, as in "I am a father" or "I am an aunt."

It may take some effort to change how you think of yourself after retirement. Just the change from "I am a mechanic" to "I was a mechanic" is a recognition of the past, of growing older. "I work for Ford Motor Company" becomes "I worked for Ford Motor Company." This subtle difference will strike at the core of who you are—an acknowledgment that your past life is not *now*. You are growing older.

When you engage in activities after retirement, your self-concept will change to include your present activities. "I am volunteering," "I am taking classes," or "I am enjoying time for myself." I was amazed that, after retirement, few people asked or were interested in my past profession. They wanted to know me now, in my present activities. I was asked, "What are you doing?" It was a painful interlude for a while, as I had no answer to the question.

Personalities will probably not change. We are still kind, solicitous, generous, impulsive, withdrawn, or quiet. Most personality characteristics are consistent throughout the life span. Who we are and how we act are related to our social world, personal relationships, and even our health status. We know personality traits *can* change. Fearfulness can be allayed; anxiety can be understood; grouchiness and negativity can be unlearned. We also have seen that love itself may soften the feelings and the person (Dittmann-Kohl 2005).

The Stress of Health Problems

As stated at the beginning of this chapter, my retirement began with a bang—a life-threatening illness. Twenty years later, I am still here and give thanks to the medical personnel who served me so well and to my family who were there with me. I was not alone in beginning retirement with illness. Others begin it alone and unprepared. For example: One morning, a woman friend received a telephone from the police. Her husband, an engineer, was discovered by the police early one morning driving down a highway the wrong way. Dressed in pajamas, he presented a sorry picture. He did not know his name or address. He was not inebriated. Rather, he was suffering from a cerebral vascular stroke. He was sixty-six years old and actively employed. What a traumatic beginning to life without work! And what a trauma for his wife!

This gives us pause to recognize that health problems are almost inevitable. Health can become a major stressor.

By the age of seventy-five, statistics indicate the following:

- Eighty-eight percent of persons have one chronic health condition; 20 percent have more than one. (Hypertension, arthritis, and heart disease are the most common chronic ailments.)[vii]

- Ninety-two percent wear glasses; 35 percent of men and 22 percent of women have some trouble hearing with one or both ears.[viii]

These are sobering statistics. None really anticipate illness. But the stress of a health condition comes with age. There are ways of managing stress that are discussed in a later chapter. For now, let us look at the emotional reactions to health problems.

Example: My retirement, which began with a life-defying illness, required undergoing six months of treatment. It seems like a dream now, and I was in a dreamlike state then. It was a strange time with long treatment sessions at the hospital and hourlong drives back and forth. Eating and sleeping just happened. Surely, I must have read books. I had excellent care from my brother and his wife. Gradually, life improved, and I teased the doctor, asking him to make me better so I could take a trip to Europe in six months' time. Thanks to the thoughtful care and expertise of the medical professionals, I did recover, and I did make that trip.

The first step in reacting to an illness is to accept it—and then, of course, to get the best medical care available. Finding out you have an illness may bring shock or disbelief; then the shock is followed by fear and anxiety. Guilt and anger are common reactions when you think you could have done something to avoid or delay the illness. An emotional temptation might be to become depressed, to think of death, or to get lost in self-pity. These attitudes do not help the healing or recovery process.

Accepting the illness means acknowledging it, finding out as much as you can about your own condition, and then making any changes in lifestyle that will make the best of it.

Jane, a seventy-year-old lady, fell on her back in an apartment where she lived alone. After crawling to the telephone, she was taken to the hospital and suffered surgery. She was determined she would walk again—and walk without needing a cane or a walker. Normally a frank, strong, and independent person, she used these qualities for her recovery. Within a month, she was walking alone, occasionally using a walker when the distance was long. She really had determination—and obstinacy. She wanted to get well.

There is also sadness when facing an illness or any bad event. Temporary sadness is expected. But then you—we—must do all in our power to take active steps to combat the illness. It has been shown that people with a pessimistic attitude are more likely to focus on symptoms and rely more on doctor appointments. They limit social activities and take few actions to ensure their own health. They learn a passive helplessness—a "take care of me" attitude. This attitude may eventually settle into depression.

And now, live life to the fullest and face each new challenge with a will to do what you can. Norman Cousins once said, "Optimism does not wait on facts. It deals with prospects. Pessimism is a waste of time." It has been well demonstrated that positive thinking may help you live a longer, happier life. When you find it difficult to think positively, try the following:

- Create positive expectations of yourself, your health, and life in general. If you begin to think negatively or expect a bad outcome, immediately change it into a positive one and speak it out loud or write it down.
- Use humor: read jokes or listen to comedies on television.
- Enjoy friendship and love. Go out of your way to find reasons to laugh and to spend time with people you like.
- Appeal to a higher power and/or use your spirit of life and contentment to provide you hope.

There will be times of illness during this period of life. You will discover that the occurrence can enhance your enjoyment of each day. Each day becomes special. It can bring a sense of exuberance that you still enjoy life. Let gratitude enter your spirit for all the joy, love, and caring you have shared.

Retirement is a good time in life. There is substantial potential for physical and mental fitness. The current emphasis on exercise and movement to keep the body healthy and strong is important for mental and physical health. It is a good time to learn new things for exercising the mind. Occasional forgetting words or names are sometimes bothersome—and sometimes funny. Generally, high levels of emotional and social well-being persist during this period. Importantly, there is time for enjoying family and friendships without a need to be responsible for everything.

Time is here. A time of contentment and companionship. A time of intimacy and closeness. Time with those you love is cherished. Time has revealed the importance of love.

CHAPTER 4

On the Bridge: The Age of Compassion Ages Seventy-Five to Eighty-Five

Here we are. We have crossed the borderland into retirement successfully. We have met with sickness and mourning, with joy and sadness, with laughter and tears. Time brings compassion for others' sufferings.

The irretrievable effects of time are here. At eighty-five years of age, I have experienced time, sometimes consciously, as when lonely, and other times unconsciously as it speeds by with busyness. I am now very aware that time is passing too quickly. There are friends to see, places I have never been, technology I will never understand, and ideas I will never know. Time passes. I cannot alter it. Every moment of time changes me. As I reach for a glass of water, drink, then set the glass down, the time has gone. I could not halt time even for a drink. Yeats said that if time is used correctly, it will bring harmony and legitimacy to life.

> And the days are not full enough
> And the nights are not full enough
> And life slips by like a field mouse
> Not shaking the Grass
> (Ezra Pound, 1941)

Time has changed me. I no longer play tennis, walk in the woods, or go skiing. My balance is poor. I no longer attend a symphony or see a movie, because of hearing problems. These are such small things in life and such big things. And my experience is not unique. Most people my age have some kind of disability.

The spaces of life have also changed—both internal and external space. The spaces around me change with the variety of environments in which I find myself. From the ages of seventy-five to eighty-five, I traveled at home and abroad. I moved to a new home and an unfamiliar city. I met new people. Changes sometimes stimulate and sometimes confuse. As a result, my internal space has been filled with a plethora of feelings, thoughts, reflections, and memories. I have known pleasure and delight, loneliness and sadness, success and failure, and especially deep gratitude that life is still with me.

As in the younger stages, the phases of aging are marked by both health—physical and mental—and by years. So let me welcome you to this new phase of life as we consider health expectations, family and social relations, and personal emotional states.

Health

> Not even lucid wisdom will give you joy
> when sacred health is gone
> (Simonides)

It is not unusual to have health difficulties during these years. No longer is improved health to be anticipated because youth and growth are long gone. We are visitors to the doctor's office because of the chronic problems that beset us. The major ailments include heart diseases, cancer, diabetes, stroke, arthritis, respiratory diseases, and Alzheimer's disease. As one lady remarked, "My social engagements are visiting doctors' offices."

Let me share a few statistics. The average older person in this phase has developed more than two chronic health problems. By eighty-five years of age, 90 percent have a chronic ailment and 20 percent have five or more illnesses when adding visual, hearing, and balance difficulties to those mentioned above.[ix] If we compare the numbers previously given for the sixty-five to seventy-five-year-old phase, we see that an additional 30–40 percent of older persons have incurred a chronic illness of some kind during this period (Crist and Dewan 2000).

The statistics are sobering. They do not reflect wishes or dreams of a healthy, long life. Yet aging is a natural process. Becoming aware of the processes within us will help adjustment to the changes we will be making. The emotional challenges are multiplied when we become ill. Enduring pain with quiet acceptance is difficult. As one sage stated, "It is all right to have pain, not to suffer with it."

Well-being has a circular path. Health is closely linked with our emotional state. In turn, feelings have a powerful impact on physical and mental vitality. Emotional life is energized by physical activity. These building blocks of life work together in close harmony—each one affecting the other.

Feelings of hope and trust enable healing. If you can meet physical and health problems with an attitude that you can manage them, your positive attitude will open the pathways to accepting and adjusting to the difficulties. You cannot see as well? Eyeglasses help. Hearing is a problem? Hearing aids let you enjoy the social world again. Balance or walking is difficult? A cane or walker or a motorized scooter can keep you mobile. For illnesses? Do what the medical doctor recommends.

First, "the proportion of elderly who are disabled is *decreasing* and the chronological age at which the majority ... have multiple functional impairments *increasing*" (Dr. habil. Jacqui Smith 2000). This means that more persons can anticipate a healthier old age; as we live longer, there is a good possibility that we may be healthier.

The current emphasis on keeping fit has come about gradually. It is now well documented that decline in functional abilities is not related to the aging process alone. The expected decline in function—including decreased muscle strength, declining respiratory capacity, and restrictions of motion—closely mimics the results of physical inactivity in our sedentary culture. For instance, a sedentary seventy-five to eighty-five-year-old person requires more than half their reserve strength simply to shower. The decline in oxygen consumption is over 12 percent throughout these years. For those who exercise regularly—such as running, bicycling, exercising, and so on—there is only a 5 percent decrease (Phillips and Davidoff 2007).

They also point out that those who exercised developed only one-fourth as many disabilities. Exercise appears to reduce high blood pressure, improve bone health, decrease the risk of falls, improve heart functioning, and in general help to maintain a healthy body. The added benefits are that it improves the emotional moods and, more especially, helps maintain a healthy mind.

I remember with a smile that when I was younger, in my thirties, I liked to run after a day of teaching—it just felt good. But I had to run at dusk, for the neighbors thought something was wrong if they saw a young lady running along the street!

Not even illness marks the end of living. Illness need not rob anyone of life or enjoyment. Difficulty in hearing need not destroy hope, the inability to walk does not necessarily immobilize, and the illness that besets one is not necessarily fatal. Take each step with an attitude that embraces hope, gratitude for the care, a smile for each person, love for each day, and humorous anticipation of what may happen next in your life.

The emotional challenge is to prepare answers for these questions: How will an illness or disability make me feel? How can I manage pain? What takes my attention away from any pain? What changes could make life easier for me? For others in my life? What exercises will strengthen me? Who and what brings humor and good feelings to me? How can I be grateful and patient with those who help me?

Social-Emotional Relationships

Relationships with Spouse/Partner

This is no borderland. By all accounts, we are older citizens. Now, during these years, relationships will narrow in focus and settle on your spouse (if still with you), your family, your close friends, and perhaps a familiar organization, such as a church.

When I see an older couple smiling at each other or holding hands while walking, the warmth they share spreads outward. Their comfort with each other is obvious. Being together with your partner brings its own rewards. Conflict issues are for the most part gone. Days are comfortably patterned. The love you share is deepened by time together.

Quiet evenings of togetherness are cherished. Even providing physical care for each other during times of illness strengthens the bond, making time together sweeter.

Time has resolved many irregularities in a relationship. When working together, and for each other, time has brought an awareness of the constancy of the other, a healing of problematic events, a mutuality of family ties with children and grandchildren, and a dependency on each other. The warmth grows; a sense of gratitude for the partner—just for their presence—brings a tenderness of feelings. Contentment is deep.

On the other hand, when disappointment, distrust, or anger has simmered between a couple for years, time does not resolve the damage and hurt. Conflicts that have remained bitter will push the couple further apart. The last years together become acrid and hostile.

Example: One couple that I counseled had been married for more than sixty years. They had three children, all successful, with families of their own. Now, at this age in life, they could hardly abide each other's company. He was a passive, nongiving, mumbler in speech. She had long given up on love and become disappointed, angry, and demanding. She had wanted them to have counseling several times earlier in their marriage; now he wanted it. Their days were a chaotic emotional tumble. His passivity was met with her anger; her anger with his withdrawal—all because of seemingly unimportant words or actions. They lived in a senior citizen community that required them to sit at the same table. They would don a smiling facade for dining. They were an unhappy couple, never to realize the contentment or love that both sought.

The difficulties of their past could not be resolved in counseling—or even brought to the surface. The conflicts and bitterness were too old, too encapsulated in their hearts, and too much a part of them to unfold the origins or meanings of their disappointments. Instead, together we arranged a schedule in which their days could become more comfortable together. The days were structured: a rising time, time for each to be alone, for eating together, for activity in the evening, and even for bedtime (which had been a major source of trouble). Hostilities lessened with the schedule, and some peacefulness came for them and between them.

Oh yes, stress may still arise during this period, especially when one or both persons are anxious. Older patterns of feelings and behavior resurface. Even so, patience, compassion, and a word of love can quiet these old feelings. These emotional reactions may be effaced with a change of attitude and expectations. What wishes do you two share that are not fulfilled? For yourself? For your partner? Have you shared them with each other? How can you help each other through times of anxiousness? Of stress? Of illness? What plans have you made together to care for each other?

Relationships with the Family

As parents and grandparents, we are the center of family traditions. For example: In my family, the main holidays were spent with my parents. I would travel by car or train from Colorado to Ohio, to be home for Christmas; my brother and his family drove about two hundred miles, arriving about midnight with their sleepy children; other siblings and their families lived closer. Christmas Eve, Thanksgiving dinner, and summer picnics were times of togetherness—even when the numbers grew to be over thirty. And, yes, as grandparents we are the center of the family—even if only one of us still lives.

You are special to your grandchildren. Not only is the relationship with you one that will guide them throughout their lives, but it is also a pattern for their own aging. You become the keeper of the culture for the family. Memories of the past come more easily and should be used. Telling the stories of past experiences to your children and grandchildren lets them know you better. More importantly, it lets them learn more about life. Singing "Over the river and through the woods ... the horse knows the way to carry the sleigh" at Thanksgiving made sense to your parents, even though they never rode on a horse-drawn sleigh. For you, it was only a fun song. Your grandchildren may find it magical.

Such memories and personal stories enter family lore. For instance, my father told the story of emigrating from Sweden as a teenager. He boarded the ship with one bag of apples for eating during the two-week journey. Another time, a creek flooded into our home, filling the basement with water. As I remember, he waded into the basement to turn off the electricity! I still have no idea how he did it without being electrocuted, but it is a story passed down as a heroic tale through four generations now.

Now, during this phase, changes will come. The family meetings become too much; preparing the meals, tolerating the noise of the children and grandchildren, and getting the house ready become difficult. Children help, then gradually take over. Usually, one child is most helpful. Roles with children are different. We become more the recipient of care than the caregiver. They may still ask for guidance or opinion on some problems in their lives, but they are adults themselves by now. Time with them is sharing their lives with their families. Gradually, the older-generation persons become more passive participants in family get-togethers. Talking, watching, and commenting on their activity. Enjoying the life around us.

Adult children become concerned about the parent's well-being—they are solicitous, helpful, and even controlling. Failing vitality and health may bring family dissension, especially when health problems arise. For example, should the parent be driving a car? Should someone accompany them to the doctor's office? Should the parent drive or go out at night? Does the parent remember to take medicines?

A family meeting was called by my oldest sister. We were to discuss whether my mother's driving license should be taken from her. She was ninety. Six of seven siblings were present. Mother's greatest pleasure was driving one mile, in a rural community, to get a frosty freeze. Despite my sister's concern, we decided that there was no reason to deprive her of this pleasure. She was healthy and able. She drove until three months before her death, safely.

During these times, emotional challenges for an aging person include: How can I listen to children's suggestions without losing control of my own life? How can I keep an open mind about what is best for me? How can I make it easier on myself and the adult child? These questions can be pondered before the necessity arises.

I have heard many adults wish they had talked more with their parents about their earlier lives. Now is the time to share personal memories with children. Or write them down. Could a chronicle be made for children and heirs? A family history? Can we tell them of our unfulfilled dreams? Can we tell them about the problems we faced and how they were handled?

Social and Community Relationships

Diminishing social relations and activities comes about gradually, sometimes because of waning interest or because of disability. Older persons fatigue more easily and become more cautious in movements and even more rigid in making plans. Even a social butterfly slows down. In this gradual detachment from people, there is more satisfaction being with those whom we know well and share interests and activities. We care more deeply about them and appreciate the part they have played in our life.

On the personal level, detachment extends to letting go of a sense of self-importance—in family and community interactions. We accept the relativity of life events. Younger people have the reins now. This attitude brings detachment from a desire to control others or situations, even if we see their errors. We watch with interest how they manage the situations, amazed at their skills. Without the responsibility, satisfaction increases as we watch others take over the reins. A sense of contentment pervades our spirit.

The Age of Compassion

This is the *age of compassion*. We have lived through pleasant joys of life and sad, difficult situations. We have known successes and failures. We have solved some problems and left some unsolved. We know love and have felt hate. We have felt regret and dismay, thinking of those we have injured. We let ourselves know the joy we have given others. We recognize the potential destructiveness of all humans; we acknowledge it within ourselves.

By knowing ourselves, our successes and failures, our strengths and weaknesses, we have an understanding of the difficulties that other suffer as well. Compassion. A desire to help is in the soul, to alleviate the discomfort you see about you—in the community and in the world. A vision comes—to see a world devoid of hunger, poor health, or killing. Simone de Beauvoir said, "One's life has value so long as one attributes value to the life of others." We feel that too.

Because so few of us live in small towns where the needs of our neighbors are easy to recognize, organizations have been developed to provide help to one another. The unhappy plight of others brings a desire to help, to do what we can. Many community agencies that provide help to others are possible only through volunteers who bring their expertise and experience to work with the community's needs.

Being a volunteer brings many advantages. It provides the opportunity to use our skills with people and situations; it gives a sense of satisfaction that enhances our self-esteem; it is gratifying to know we can be helpful. A side benefit is that we meet new and often interesting people. Showing compassion and warmheartedness may also reduce blood pressure, anxiety, and stress and, in general, improve health.

Some challenging questions include the following: How can we replace some of our loneliness with time spent contributing to others? How can we participate—even with the depletion of energy? How may we make new friendships, if desired?

I have saved the best for last. Surely, the loss of our partner, of our parents, or of some friends causes sadness and mourning. Surely, we miss them. Some we miss more dearly every day.

Surely, we have known the sense of losing control over parts of our life or even our physical being. This lets us watch the world go on. Surely, we have all suffered—and known the toll that takes on our life.

But with the freedom from responsibility, inner freedom may develop that opens a different, wider world. We can take classes in subjects that have long interested us; we can travel to parts of the world we have only heard or read about; we can talk to people we have not known; or we can visit museums that we previously passed by. As a result, we notice things about ourselves as if we had new eyes and new ears. Our senses, while somewhat depleted, are more sensitive; we notice things that have passed by us in our former hurried life. New interests catch our attention. We see connections missed before—spirituality, philosophy, and everyday living. Nature becomes a metaphor for our own living and dying; flowers, trees, weather, and animals share existence.

It is important to note that recent studies have shown that intelligence does not inevitably decline among the mentally alert and healthy elderly. This is especially true in areas such as understanding of and insight into problem situations, creative understanding, and metaphorical thinking (Baltes 2003).

For me, after a period of ten years of illness and caretaking of others, the world seemed to open! I found myself writing poetry—never even thought of that before. I began to contribute articles to a local magazine. I met the most interesting people!

I was breathing freely! Like breathing in the fresh air after a rain. I could not breathe deeply enough of it. I watched little birds with fascination. Even pebbles on the lawn caught my attention with their varied colors and shapes. Butterflies reminded me of ideas that float through the air—not always to be caught, only to be shared. Life was good, and a sense of deep joy filled me—elation unknown in earlier living.

Creativity is closely tied to spirituality and the search for the meaning of life itself. Philosophical and spiritual thoughts become frequent as one considers the meaning of life and of what life, if any, follows death. Spiritual pursuits and formal religions provide solace for many during this period. The quest for peace and contentment helps us evolve an inner acceptance of life and of death.

Yet at this age, we are nearing the end. Each day brings the time of death nearer. Do I think of dying? Of course. These are not morbid thoughts—only a little sadness that life has gone so quickly. An increasing number of us are living longer, healthier, and more active—even until the age of one hundred. We now turn to this last phase.

Time is like a leaf in the wind; it is a phantom. Time has come and gone, yet there is more time to come—at least today is here. Time has ripened the substance of life; it is here now. Time has not gone. Can you hear time passing by?

Chapter 5

The Curtain Call—The Encore Ages Eighty-Five Plus

The older we grow, the greater becomes our ordeals.
—Goethe

Time. Time is all. No time. Time is today only. I cannot count on more time. Memories of time passed now persist. Life has been so short. Yesterday I was skipping rope with friends. Ah, my first kiss with the boy next door. College was fun. Time to remember. Time is gone. Waiting. Waiting for the curtain call. Alone.

We have lived long—eighty-five years and more. We honor each moment. Moments are more important than ever, for the moment is ours. To be present observing, listening, participating, and mostly feeling. We have learned that the meaning of any moment resides in how it makes us feel.

The past is within me. Reminiscing fills some moments. There are pleasant memories of love, loving, acceptance and friendship, and achievements; the strongest is the warmth of love. There are painful memories; regretted choices, failures, and disappointing others; waves of anger and fears; hatred; the sadness of the loss of family and friends; and stressful days that aged us. All these are part of me. They define who I am. Your memories are there with you too, defining the person you became and are.

At eighty-five plus, the future is uncertain. We cannot be sure of the day to come. Living is now. For me, I greet each day with a smile—even a broader smile when the sun is shining and the birds are singing. I want to be here. I am glad to be here. I anticipated that life would grow easier and less stressful. That does not seem to be the case. With growing older, more is expected. We are asked to change our habits and behaviors to fit our living situation, to adapt to limitations in movement and in our ability to care for ourselves, to become dependent on the services of others, and to accept our state with ease, dignity, and grace.

There is much to figure out and decide, such as the following: Who am I? Where will I live out my days? How will my children treat me? Will my grandchildren like me or respect me? Will I end up alone, without friends or family? How will my health be? How can I be happy as I become older?

Who Are We?

I protest the thought that we are different because we are old. I feel the same as I did when younger. We have lived longer than most people. We are the oldest old of our culture. Just imagine, there were about two million persons in the United States over eighty-five years of age in 2010; we make up less than 2 percent of the population. About three-fourths of us are women, and most are widows (84 percent). Only 6.3 percent of women are still married; however, over 43 percent of men have wives with them; one half of the men are widowers.[x] What a privilege to have been granted life for these years!

Ninety-plus years ago, in 1921, a longevity project began at Stanford University. It has followed the same people and their lives throughout these years. It found that participants who lived the longest were noted for their conscientiousness, thoughtful choices, and being able to establish and maintain social relationships even in their childhood (Friedman and Martin 2011, p. 182). Perhaps as we look at our own lives, we have some sense of whether these characteristics fit. Thankfully, I think they fit many.

It turns out that the quality of social involvement we have is the most consistent and significant factor that emerges in studies of longevity. Those who lived this long seem to fall into three personality groups: the solitary ones, the social ones, and the discontented ones.

The Solitary Ones

We have talked about Patricia before as an adventurer/craftsperson who fulfilled her lifetime dreams, even buying a horse when she was in her seventies. She is now eighty-seven years old and has lived alone in her house for eighteen years. When she first retired, she would become so preoccupied with art projects that she would work into the wee hours of the night—painting, wood carving, ceramics, and so on. At this age, she is spending her days alone, occasionally returning to her artistic work. She takes an afternoon nap and watches television or plays games on her computer. She is relatively healthy but is aware of increasing problems with her memory. She is not a hermit, for she has a small group of friends who meet to have dinner together or play card games. She will not consider moving into a retirement community, because there are too many people, not enough space for her artistic endeavors, and too many restrictions. She loves her solitude.

Patricia's solitude is only one variation. Here is a different story. Susan died alone at the age of ninety-five. She was a wealthy, renowned architect. She lived alone for twenty-five years after her husband died, had no relatives, and had only one friend. She refused any professional help, such as social services, meal delivery, or live-in help. Nor would she consider moving to a group setting, as an assisted-living organization. She suffered from severe back problems and could hardly move about. Her last two years were lived in bed with a carton of Ensure and a clutter of financial papers and reports with her. I asked if I could get her books to read; she responded that she did not read books. But she did read and study complicated financial reports! Intelligent, yes. Alone, yes. She had no remaining social contacts, and none were desired.

Patricia and her neighbor are both in a group that maintained a high level of cognitive performance. These loners have personal goals and interests that occupy their thinking, problem-solving, and time. They thrive with time alone to pursue these interests; they want and need solitude. Their social relations focus on a small group of friends who provide pleasant interaction and social stimulation for them. When those friends are gone, no one is there.

The Social Ones

This second group is made up of persons who enjoy people and usually have a large social network. These people thrive in social settings. Often, the more people, the merrier. They have a disposition to enjoy life and seek almost constant social relationships. Reading books usually does not hold their interest, nor do they have hobbies to fill alone time. Their intelligence is good, but they have not developed much intellectual curiosity. They are happy with a wide circle of friends and many social activities. When alone, they tend to get anxious or depressed.

For example: Kim, aged ninety, was a very sociable person, with many friends. She is the mother of three children, eight grandchildren, and eight great-grandchildren. She enjoys the families and visits with them a couple of days every week. Her arthritis is becoming worse, and she moves about with a walker. She lives alone in a senior residential center. Here she is surrounded by people playing bridge, working on puzzles, and participating in most activities. In her earlier days, she was a leader of several groups in her church, participated in community walks for different health programs, had lunch with different friends, and belonged to a group that played bridge. She was the fun of the party and able to put others at ease and to engage them in activities. Kim now prefers to sit in the lounge where others are sure to join her. At mealtimes, she is aware of anyone who is absent or having difficulties. She is known for her sense of humor and her love for talking with everyone.

While Kim seems a social butterfly, there are others in this group whose lives are more invested in social service functions and who utilize their energies in helping others. They have often developed a community and worldview to life that provides purpose and meaning.

Ellen, aged eighty-five, thrives on social contact. She has invested her life in service to the community. She leads a weekly prayer group, volunteers in community programs for the homeless, and is recognized as the person to see for guidance and wisdom. She has written guidelines that summarize her personal philosophy and spiritual beliefs. She still lives in her apartment, alone. But at least three days a week, she breakfasts with friends. A busy woman even yet, she has geared her activities toward leadership in spiritual activities.

These persons remain social and involved in activities. Their vitality is maintained through meeting the needs of others. They are the mothers of all.

The Discontented Ones

This third group possesses a somewhat lower level of functioning. They have a strong dependence on others, both psychological and physical. For them, there is a notable decrease in cognitive functioning during this period. Their relationships with others are often catastrophic, based on their needs not being met, many complaints of physical ailments, and an inability to be satisfied. Nothing is good enough. Their lives are marked by loneliness and a lack of interest in living.

Ben was a retired barber. At the age of eighty-eight, his main topic of conversation was the "good old days." Although he could regale one with interesting stories, his conversation focused on how awful life had been since he retired.

He reluctantly moved into the home of his daughter and her husband after his wife died. He suffers from arthritis, a back problem because of years of standing. It has not disabled him, although he walks with a cane. He is also hard of hearing but wears his hearing aid when reminded. His main activity is watching television. He constantly complains about the announcers, the commercials, or the program themselves. He will not change programs, even though complaining. He does not like to read and has no hobbies. He hates doctors but often finds an additional pain to see one. He is disgruntled, and nothing is good enough: his daughter does not give him the right food, the grandchildren are too noisy, the doctors don't help his pain, and so on. He constantly demands attention, but nothing is good enough. He does not want to die, yet life is not good for him. As his pain becomes worse, he is more dependent on his daughter and her husband. Yet nothing they do or offer satisfies him. He does not want to see friends—that is, if any are still alive.

Ben has always been discontented with life. It did not happen with getting older or weaker. His aging simply helped him focus more on himself than on things happening at home or in the world. To understand Ben's complaining and grumbling is to realize he has not taken responsibility for himself; nor has he developed a sense of gratitude for life or for others who care. The discontent may cover deep fears of abandonment and may be used to combat depression. But it makes it very difficult for family or caretakers to be with them.

Where Do We Live?

These years find us with significantly fewer family relations and significantly fewer social relationships. Where we live often determines the frequency of contact with others, the depth of our relationships, the breadth of our conversations, participation in situations and events, and our sense of well-being.

The oldest old live in a variety of places—some we choose and some without choice. About one-third of us live alone; one-third live in a household with relatives or unrelated individuals; about one-fourth live in an institutional setting with skilled nursing facilities. Men live with relatives (53 percent) more often than women do (32 percent). Caucasian senior citizens are almost twice as likely to live alone as Asians or Hispanics. Almost all rely on Social Security, with about half living at the poverty level.[xi]

Living with Our Family

One-third of older persons live with family. For some cultures and families, it is expected that aging parents will live with their children. Three generational homesteads are common and anticipated as part of life. In this setting, the adult child gradually takes over more of the parental responsibilities as aging parents become less able. A family is an integrated unit; they share the home.

However, in our culture, most couples have moved into their own homes with their own children. When parents age and/or become ill, and especially when finances are limited, it may be necessary to share a home to provide care. Many adult children are not emotionally prepared to take over responsibility for their parents. As these changes occur, it can be stressful for both generations. It is an adjustment for all as everyone experiences a change in roles and in expectations of one another.

When living with children, roles change. No longer the patriarch or matriarch, older parents are now relegated to a more passive role. We watch others do what we used to do. This may be difficult. But a feeling of gratitude can be cultivated for the safety and security that is given. A warm appreciation can develop for the love, care, and work that others provide.

For all, despite the challenges, the time together brings an opportunity to know one another more intimately.

One patient, Maria, a professional woman in her fifties, came for counseling when situations compelled her to bring her mother into her home. Her mother was in the early stages of Alzheimer's disease and could no longer live alone. Maria had never developed warm feelings for her mother and, for many reasons, had moved far away. Now she had little choice; her mother needed care. As the disease became worse, Maria faced many stressful days—and some humorous ones. One day, Maria was telephoned by the local bank. Her mother had cut out a check from a magazine and was trying to cash it!

When her mother died two years later, Maria reported that those two years with her mother were among the best in her life. They talked, they shared memories, they had dinner together each day, and Maria learned to love and appreciate her mother as she learned her mother's life story. Early disappointments were erased with understanding.

Living in a Residence for Senior Citizens

A third of the old-old are living in some type of residential setting. Many are alone, without spouses, siblings, or children. Living in a residence does provide daily interaction with others and often additional activities as well. The comradeship that comes with the mutuality of age, with a general acceptance of weakness and disabilities of aging, and with shared aloneness is often opening for friendships—for sharing life stories and interests.

An example: Mary, a friend ninety-four years old, had been living alone after her husband died. In her loneliness and grief, she became increasingly depressed. For over a year, her daughter tried to convince Mary to move closer. Mary was very reluctant to leave her home and neighborhood. It would mean another loss, and the potential strangeness frightened her. Finally convinced, Mary agreed. Her daughter found an apartment in a residential setting for seniors. Soon, Mary made friends; her daughter could visit her regularly; her depression disappeared. Mary reported that the move, while stressful, had made her aware that there were others who shared a similar fate as hers. She easily found friends, and together they engaged in activities of the center. Mary found that life could still be pleasant.

In residential settings, friendships may flourish and relieve the loneliness and the aloneness of the old-old. The settings often offer programs and excursions that encourage contact with the greater social environment. These living arrangements have the advantage of providing stimulation that may be missing within family settings. It has been found that individuals who engage in interaction with a wider variety of social partners and interact relatively less with family members have better language skills and better cognitive function. This is especially true of those who have lived in a residential setting for a longer period.

Limiting conversation to one's family seems to be particularly *disadvantageous:* the higher the proportion of interactions with family, the poorer the cognitive and language performances become (Keller-Cohen et al. 2006). Interactions with family are routine, cover similar conversational topics, and provide less stimulation. Also, the extent of shared experiences and understanding among family members is so great that the older person may not need to work very hard to communicate.

While our sense of well-being is more dependent upon close family relations, friendships may be more important for our morale and our vigor. There are strong indications that there may be important benefits to living independently in an age-congregate residential environment.

Living Alone

About 33 percent of the old-old persons live alone, whether in a home of many years or an apartment setting. The reasons for being alone are many—not all by choice. Some persons want to stay in their home; it is familiar and comfortable, and they feel safe and secure. The thought of moving is frightening. Some live alone because they are alone—without family. Some cannot tolerate the stress of relocating or thoughts of giving up possessions, which is often a necessity. Others have psychological forces that constrain them from moving—even into an independent-living situation. And many, many feel alone even when living in an apartment designed for senior citizens.

Example: Ella, aged ninety-three, lived alone for over forty years. She was a talented musician. She became a solitary person and neglected her musical achievements after suffering a physically abusive husband and enduring a bitter rejection by professional friends, she became increasingly frightened of further social involvement, and withdrew from relationships with others. She found contentment and some happiness in listening to the music of others and living in solitude. Although alone, she maintained close contact with a male friend and an aunt throughout her life.

Ella could not tolerate the idea of being in proximity to others because of the traumas she had endured. She was too frightened even to attend a movie theater.

Then there is Bridget. Bridget is eighty-seven years old. She has a son and a daughter, both living about nine hundred miles away. She loves her children and grandchildren, but she does not see them often. She feels she would become a burden if she were to move closer to them; that idea seems horrid to her, for she spent many young years caring for her parents and does not wish that upon her children. She has made a life for herself that involves friends and activities. Although she talks about loneliness and is lonely at times, she is comfortable where she is. She has not given much thought to aging or possible illness, feeling that she will manage that when it comes.

So often, living alone has just happened because of deaths and losses, disabilities, or financial concerns. Many who live alone experience intense loneliness. They have outlived relatives and friends. They face life and death on their own.

Living in the Hospice Setting

Many, many may spend those final days in a nursing home, in which social interactions are limited because of the severe illnesses that have come. Good care is there, given by devoted and committed caregivers. It is a time of aloneness. I love the story told about one man in a nursing home. He had some strength yet did not help the staff with the process of bathing and dressing. When questioned about this, he responded that if he dressed himself, he would have no energy left to go to the community room and be with other people! This seemed fine, wise conservation of his energy resources.

Health Challenges

Health is not predictable, especially in these later years. I am reminded of my uncle. Although he was eighty-one years old, he felt hale enough to plant a tree for his daughter. Yet his strength did not last; he collapsed while shoveling the dirt, preparing to set the tree in the ground. Accepting the timeline of life becomes an important emotional task in these years. The end is coming. The aches and pains, the slowness and shakiness, the dependent-independent struggles forebode the end. And ye, at age eighty-five, the odds are good that many will live to be ninety-one years old.[xii]

But probably not on your own, because during these ages:

- Sixty-eight percent need help with errands, such as shopping, doctors' appointments, and so on.
- Sixty-six percent have difficulty walking and climbing stairs or have balance problems.
- Forty-five percent have problems dressing or bathing.
- Forty percent have cognitive problems as memory or problem solving.
- Forty-three percent have severe hearing problems.

Yet limitations are not inevitable. A few seem not to have any disability or ailments and live well enough on their own. There have been many efforts to understand the relationship between healthfulness, personality traits, and quality of social relationships. For instance, heart failure, chronic pulmonary disorder, osteoporosis, and depression are less disabling when the senior citizen has a sense of inner strength, resilience, and self-transcendence.[xiii] Time and again, the studies of aging persons suggest that how one feels about health is more important than objective health measures in predicting long-term health (Zoon et al., p. 348). That is, whether one may focus on illness or emphasize health in daily life is an important driving force for life. A positive attitude restrains a person from overreacting to aches and pains. It accepts the illness or disability; it searches for the best medical provisions but does not let it rule life. This person is engaged in continuing life's activities as much as possible.

There are those who make a catastrophe of every illness. These persons are miserable, blaming the medical profession and the care they receive for their aches and pains, or bad luck. They go for medical care for each pain yet are never satisfied. Nor do they follow medical suggestions for good health.

It is important to recognize that the pathway to healthful living is a highly individual matter. Genetic inheritance plays a role, yet equally important are a person's attitude and emotional approach to life and the paths followed along the way.

A Hopeful Perspective

To acknowledge the arc of life's path is an emotional task in these years. Adapting to the challenges of older ages requires a constant acceptance of changes in health and life situations. New pains may emerge every day; the stairway may take longer to climb; it may be more difficult to bathe or dress.

My uncle, a defiantly independent soul, reported that it took him all morning to get dressed—not only because his movements were slower but also because the pain seemed different each day. He did not want any help! I both admire his persistence and wish he had permitted himself to have help.

Life is good for those who have a sense of well-being and accept their pathway, whatever it brings. They claim happiness and hold a positive outlook, especially if they are relatively free of pain and regardless of some difficulties. It is important to be aware that recent studies have shown that intelligence does not inevitably decline among the mentally alert and healthy elderly. This is especially true in areas such as comprehension of and insight into problem situations, in creative understanding, and in metaphorical thinking (Baltes 2003).

After all, Goethe completed *Faust* at the age of eighty-eight, Sophocles wrote *Oedipus at Colonus* at age eighty-nine, Titian painted masterpieces at age ninety-eight, Justice Holmes was writing Supreme Court decisions at ninety, and Benjamin Franklin was helping frame the American Constitution at age eighty. And let's not forget the pictures of Grandma Moses, who painted late into her life of 101 years. There are many others, too many to cite. Old age need not be a decline! It is a challenge; it is time.

Even centenarians report that life is good, although they experience difficulties in taking care of themselves. Most centenarians have health limitations. Those in better health tend to be optimistic; those with more health problems realistically report their health is not good, the quality of their life is poor, and they have little hope for improvement. They accept their downhill path.

Well-Being in These Years

What is well-being during these years? Time has brought us from the dependent infant to the relatively dependent older senior citizen. Well-being represents different feelings at different ages. For those in this encore phase, well-being refers to a good quality of life, a state of contentment, and low levels of distress.

There are several characteristics of well-being that may help keep that inner feeling that life is and has been good. I am convinced that, whatever our age, we can maintain a good feeling of life and our place in it. I am also convinced that whatever the past, at this age, we can use these feelings to make our days pleasant—at least within ourselves. The following attributes seem an essential part of well-being for us: (1) safety and security, (2) acceptance, (3) resilience, (4) reminiscence, and (5) positive attitude.

Safety and security. A sense of safety and security, both internally and in the environment, are necessities throughout our life and especially during these years when we are less able to depend on ourselves and less able to manage our own lives. It can also elicit the greatest fear and cause the most stress.

An easy, helpful means of maintaining a sense of inner safety and security is to develop a schedule for the day and even for the week. Habits are useful, guiding our next movements. However, be prepared to change them easily when new situations arise.

There are some major decisions that affect a sense of security. It is possible, even necessary, to make some of these decisions before they become necessary, such as the following: Where will you be living—with relatives and/or in a professional care setting? Who will take on responsibility for seeing to your well-being? Who will be there to manage financial affairs? And any other factors that seem necessary to ensure, if possible, what happens to you and the quality of care you receive. These are big questions. Our entire life experiences must be drawn on to address them.

Accept your state of being. It is imperative that a person has an inner acceptance of whatever life has given at this time. Are you ill? Disabled? First, have the best medical and/or nursing care that you can. Then accept your state of being. "Yes, I am ..." or "Yes, I have ..." Talk to yourself. Let yourself know that this is where it is for you at this stage of life. It is your job to make the best of it for yourself. It does not have to be inflicted upon others.

Are you unhappy? Accept that as your state now; then look about you with gratitude, even for the clouds. A simple smile may make you feel better.

Resilience. Resilience was mentioned earlier in this book. Resilience is that ineffable quality that lets us adjust to the most difficult situations; it is the ability to take the measure of a situation, identify the positive aspects, and accept unchangeable situations. As we age, many situations are new to us. We may have to adapt to situations and conditions that we had not imagined. It is imperative that we let ourselves go with the flow, always looking for ways we can make it better for ourselves.

Reminiscence. The older-old have memories that relive past events. It is a normal process throughout life and often helps us cope with difficult situations. In the older person, it may become more repetitive conversational material, as some cognitive powers are lost. Most, however, use reminiscence in a constructive manner. First, reminiscing about our past with children and other interested people is a way to provide a picture of who we are and how we met life's challenges. Reminiscences provide a reflection of the high point of our lives. It is a means to preserve our personal history and a history of our cultural times.

Reminiscence has even more value. It is a search to understand our lives, to find an awareness of who we have been and are. From infancy, I always had hearing difficulties. It has only been in reminiscing with my brother that I understood the full effects this had on my personality and social life. I was quiet and bookish. It put my history into a new framework. Reminiscence allows a clearer meaning about us and our lives. Memories can enable the integration of our life for us. Using memories in this way leads to a sense of inner wholeness and integrity.

Positive attitude. Walt Whitman wrote, "Keep your face always toward the sunshine—and shadows will fall behind you." This is the essence of a positive attitude; it is not simplistic. It is not sticking your head in the sand. A positive attitude looks for the possibilities in the situation; it is greeting each new day with a smile. It is meeting each new person and situation with curiosity.

It is talking to yourself, keeping an inner sense that you can make the most of any challenge. When a dissonant thought or feeling comes, tell yourself that it will work out and encourage yourself. Change your thoughts to more pleasant ideas. You do not have to dwell on the dissonance in life situations.

A most important characteristic for keeping a positive outlook on life is a feeling of gratitude—gratitude for life, gratitude for others, and gratitude for professional care. A thank you brings a sense of warmth to all. And if there was one characteristic responsible for well-being at any age, it is the sense of love.

The path of life narrows in these last years. A primary feature of life, with or without others, is how we feel about the path we have taken. If gratification and satisfaction have marked the way, if love has been shared with others, if a sense of warmth pervades our being, the end may be approached with inner freedom and calmness. But if there is work to do, now may be your only chance. Live in the now and get to work.

We began this chapter with reflections on time. Are we waiting passively for time to end? Or do we keep an investment with life even in these closing days? Do we choose to live them? I am still here. The path of life guides me, with a consciousness of each moment, with gratitude for each day. I am conscious of the bird on my patio, of the seasons of flowers. I am living out time now. Time may not give me tomorrow. My life will not count more than others. Yet this time, my time, is important to me.

Part II

CHAPTER 6

Our Challenge: Caring for Ourselves

The different phases of growing older have shown differences in structure and relationships. The process of aging has been described, beginning with acceptance of retirement, through the ages of compassion, volunteerism, and companionship, to the encore years, a curtain call through reminiscence and maintaining our autonomy. We now approach some of the most difficult tasks in aging wisely.

Several studies of older persons, even descriptions of the oldest-old have suggested several characteristics that are shared by those who have lived long and well.[1] Among these are activity and exercise, a positive mindset, resilience, ability to balance stress, good self-esteem and stubbornness and close bonds with others. Other descriptions add productiveness and a sense of meaning in life.

Feelings grow stronger and clearer as we move through the stages of life. At times, those feelings become so strong that they interfere with happiness, contentment, and our relationship with others. Yet we find ways to handle these situations. It is not always the easy or the optimal way. Sometimes we rely on relatives, friends, professional services, or government services. Through it all, we need to have ways to recognize the disaster to our life and find ways of relief.

These next chapters address some of the problems that are encountered

---

[1] Michael Watson, "7 Traits the Oldest Seniors have in Common," 2016, https://www.Caring Senior Service.7 traits the oldest seniors have in common.

in these years—whether in our fifties or nineties. The chapters examine stressful topics. They focus on stones in the pathway of aging that can bruise tender feet. Knowing that these feelings are common and that there are ways we can relieve them can be helpful and contribute to a sense of well-being.

An important message for these chapters is that feelings do not disintegrate with age. They become more complex, and the expression of emotions is now tempered. Maintaining a sense of independence and control over living is a major anxiety. Confidence in coping with times of crises is important, for the loss of independence is a major stress while aging. Resolving the problems that arise in a satisfactory manner is the focus of that chapter.

Aging is not all bad. The sense of well-being can persist. We can feel good about life. Dealing with health issues may make our spirits stumble temporarily, and the resolution resounds within us.

In the following chapters, some complex situations shall be discussed and hopefully lead to better understanding for life as an older person.

Chapter 7

Are Our Emotions Growing Older?

> Let's not forget that the little emotions are the great captains
> of our lives, and we obey them without realizing it.
> —Vincent van Gogh (1889)

I used to ask my mother as she was growing older, "What do you feel? What do you feel like inside?" I wanted to know if she experienced her feelings differently now that she was older. She would respond, "I feel the same as I have always felt." It was not until I became older that I fully understood that she was saying that her feelings were the same, that she still felt gladness, sadness, and the other emotions as she always had. Aging had not changed her internal sense of self. Now I know that what she said is true.

Popular notions suggest that older folk become harder to talk to, more resistant to change, obstinate, and willful. Contrary to these myths, aging itself does not bring an increase in negative moods or unhappiness. The research suggests the opposite: there is an increase in positive feelings.

The changes in thinking and memory while growing older have been well documented. Almost everyone becomes aware of the changes in memory—especially in short-term memory. Beginning about fifty years of age, most people have been embarrassed when they forgot the name of a friend or frustrated when they forgot what they were looking for as they walked into a room. I vividly remember the first time I had difficulty recalling a technical term. I was teaching a class and stumbled to find the word. Rather than acknowledge I couldn't recall the word, I had to restart the idea all over again, beginning in a different way to express the thought. Hopefully, the lack was not noted by the class members, and the roundabout description proved more effective than a specific term.

By now, many people are acquainted with research about maintaining our health through physical activity, practicing our memory, and learning new things as a means of prolonging our capabilities. But not much information has been forthcoming about our feeling life—and this *is* our life. Despite almost noble efforts a person gives to healthful nutrition and maintaining regular exercise, the physical person changes. Aging brings a loss of vigor and of physical health and a body that fails. Emotions are not lost.

Emotional Life

Aging does not change feelings or the sense of the self. Nor does growing older diminish the intensity of feelings. Feelings remain available in their fullness throughout life. Feelings are with us from birth. Observed in infancy are happiness, surprise, anger, sadness, fear, delight, and disgust—feelings that seem necessary for life itself. For instance, happiness can be seen with that first smile, anger can be evident in many hungry cries, fear comes with a loss of physical safety, and disgust is obvious to any mother when the baby spits out food that they did not like. The basic feelings states are not lost with time. Feelings refer to bodily experience; *emotions* refer to the expression of feelings. I tend to use the words interchangeably unless a specific reference is needed.

Feelings endure. Older persons laugh at jokes, enjoy the play of grandchildren, become disgusted with slow service in the restaurant, love their partner and children, become angry at impoliteness, and smile with friends. Feelings continue to enrich the quality of life.

Feelings are our greatest friends and sometimes our worst enemies. They are our constant companions, and they govern much of what we do. They are an immediate reaction to any situation and direct our thinking and behavior. In popular jargon, a person might say they have a gut reaction to a situation—meaning that they had a feeling that something was good or not (Greenberg 2012). This is a premonition to be honored.

I had a friend, aged fifty-two, who lived alone. Walking home a few blocks at dusk, she had a feeling she was being followed by a man. She changed her pace; he seemed to change his. She varied her pace several times, becoming even more frightened—as he also did. She ran into the nearest house with lights on; he followed her. It was his home, and he had matched her pace so that he would not frighten her. Her gut reaction was a fear-arousing, self-protective reaction. She had honored her feelings. A good laugh was enjoyed. In another instance, her feeling may have provided a signal against real danger for her protection.

The Strength of Emotions

Growing older does not diminish the intensity of feelings. Research has shown that age generally does not affect how strongly we feel. In one study involving more than 1,700 persons over the age of sixty and from different cultures, it was shown that older persons experience as intense feelings as younger adults (Magai 2010, p. 410). That means we can feel as much and as deeply as we did when we were younger.

The patterns of expression and neurophysiologic reactions that are associated with feelings are well established. As aging continues, these reactions and patterns remain intact. Research has shown that generally age does not affect the autonomic responsiveness of feelings, though aging may alter the thresholds that activate an emotional response. That is, events may not trigger a response as quickly, and the response may be milder. However, even with the loss of cognitive abilities, as in Alzheimer's disease and other dementias, emotional reactions are present and observable on the face of the person (Magai, p. 422).

Emotional Growth

Intensity. Through the experiences of life, there is a deepening of emotions and a refinement of the emotional repertoire. Feelings become more complex as they are integrated with the experiences and thoughts of a lifetime. We fall in love with a special person; we like several persons, but the intensity is less. We adore our children. We *dislike* our snoopy neighbor. We hate rock-and-roll music; we love Mozart. And so on, for each basic feeling. Love becomes more finely attuned and includes feelings such as affection, tenderness, infatuation, lust, care, and so on. Anger is expressed in a variety of ways, such as irritation, exasperation, rage, disgust, envy, jealousy, and so forth.

Complexity. Our feelings become more complicated as we interact in many situations toward the same person. For instance, we may love our spouse but dislike the way he combs his hair, be proud of his patience with children, be jealous of the attention he gives to his parents, and so on. All these feelings are in us and are part of the relationship with just one person. More than one feeling may be present at the same time.

Love and anger may be directed toward the same person, as when someone we love disappoints. I remember the look on a friend's face when she was opening a gift from her husband. She hoped for a wristwatch. The gift was a watch but such a cheap one that in her emotional reactions she showed anticipation, surprise, disappointment, and anger—all were there, almost simultaneously.

Fear and love may be combined when a person is in a partnership with an abusive person. This makes it very difficult for some abused persons to leave the abusive person and/or scene of the abuse. The person is caught between wanting to be loved, a sense of guilt, and self-protective actions. Another common reaction: during grieving when a loved person dies, feelings of anger and sadness are often mixed in mourning. It is important in facing our feelings that we separate them—that is, knowing the anger and disappointment toward that person and distinguishing that from the love that was shared.

Constancy. On the fortunate side of aging, as we grow older, we tend to become more emotionally stable. Our patterns of reactions become personality characteristics as we select among useful, inappropriate, or untenable emotional reactions. For example, "I'll never do that again." With the increase in emotional balance, we are better able to solve highly emotional problems.

Coping with Feelings

Most persons develop increasing inner control and more flexibility in managing emotionally loaded situations. They learn that flying off the handle often has the opposite effect than was desired. The overall result is that the person develops a greater range of emotional responses to problematic situations. Consequently, this brings an increase in positive feelings and a corresponding lessening of negative, stress-loaded reactions.

The maturation of emotions leads to four strategies of managing feelings that are used more by older persons than middle-aged adults. These are placing the event into perspective, focusing on the positive aspects of the situation, accepting negative situations, and avoiding negative resolutions

The first advantage of coping with emotions is the ability and preference for *putting the event into a perspective.* That is, they can consider the relative importance of the event in comparison to its overall effects. Once I had a complicated situation with an aunt and uncle living with me. It was at times difficult because our personalities and style of life differed significantly. One time, my aunt wanted to rearrange the dishes in my cupboard. That I did not expect! Wanting a peaceful setting, when something happened that upset me, I learned to ask myself the question "Is *this* that important?" Was an expression of my feelings worth provoking an emotionally difficult situation? Usually, the answer to myself was no. I really did not care if she rearranged the dishes. The event was insignificant for the good life we shared.

Another instance: many older persons, as grandparents, permit the grandchildren freedoms they did not tolerate with their children. Much to the dismay of the child's parents, they protest, "You would never let me do that!" The grandparents now have a different perspective on life and understand that the activity will keep the child content and will not affect a situation in a harmful manner.

The second strategy of coping is developed through the experiences of life. It is the ability to *focus on the positive aspects* of life's situations rather than remembering, obsessing on, or emphasizing the unhappy, disturbing, or negative aspects. I have heard many an older person report, "My son does not visit me very often. That is all right because he sends me extra money every month. He is busy. I know he loves me." Thus, she focuses on his generosity and love. It makes her feel happier and more content. Of course, she would appreciate more visits but does not choose to focus on the frequency of his visits.

This positive refocusing—thinking about pleasant situations instead of the actual threatening or stressful event—is an emotional savior. To reminisce on the negative feelings would be to invite anger, sadness, or depression that would darken one's days. Paying attention to the happier, more peaceful events and memories brightens the mood, clears away the gray feelings, and often brings a lingering smile. Positive refocusing may take effort at first. To look on the bright side is easier for those who are more naturally optimistic. For those who have learned to expect the worst, it will require practice to emphasize the good and to filter out unpleasant aspects of difficult situations. Some possible ways to turn the negative into a positive focus may include the following:

- Delay a response. Whenever a disgruntled or angry response wants to be your first impulse, take a deep breath. Then ask yourself what is so frightening (or different, or ...) that you must immediately deny it with a no or with grouchiness or criticism.
- In your thinking as well as in talking, some care should be taken not to use the "but" clauses. As he is a good son, *but* he does not telephone, *but* his wife is controlling, *but* he is too busy. He is a good son—period. That will turn the thoughts and feelings toward brighter responses.
- Bite your tongue before speaking; smile and accept what is there with a "thank you" or "I don't think so, thank you."
- Before giving an answer, ask for more information or clarification, such as, "I am not sure what you mean" or "Tell me more about it."

One thing I have noticed is that many older persons prefer not to listen to much news on the television. It is too negative and too violent, and listening is emotionally upsetting. They do not want to be disturbed by the horrors, terrors, and wars of the world. They simply choose not to watch the news.

An *acceptance of the negative aspects* of a stressful event is the third coping skill managed by older adults. This is resignation to a situation we cannot alter, such as accepting the illness or disability that besets us. While this may seem a terrible way to cope, it is realistic. Consider the number of situations that none of us can alter. The key is in attitude. Resignation is not submission; it is acceptance.

One seventy-nine-year-old man was unable to walk well because of a stroke. He smiled and said to his son, "Now I get to drive around in a motor scooter—I've always wanted to try one." Stressed? Yes. Resigned? Yes. Accepted? Yes. Defeated? No.

One *unsuccessful* way to accept the negative event is through passive resignation. It is simple submission; it is giving in and giving up. It represents a powerless, defeated attitude that brings pathological passivity and depression. Another attitude is a *negative* resignation to the negative situation. Usually, this attitude is marked by active hating and fighting against the situation. These feelings make the person—and anyone around her/him—miserable with the complaints. And incidentally, it increases the distress by attending to the negative. One upside to this approach is that it may fight off depression, which could be severe.

Acceptance of the negative aspects of a stressful event is just that; then one can attempt to make the situation the best possible to meet one's needs. One eighty-nine-year-old mother who could no longer walk, get out of bed, or care for herself found herself in a hospice situation. Her response was simply "I guess this is where they place old people." She knew and accepted that death was inevitable. There was an accepting peacefulness about her that elicited the best of nursing attention.

The fourth coping skill involves *avoidance of negative situations* and is probably the easiest reaction when it is possible. With retirement and then aging, the social environment usually becomes more limited. It is then easier to avoid situations that make us uncomfortable or do not bode to be a pleasant time. Invitations to social events are more easily refused. Even more intimate social situations are often avoided, if possible.

My husband and I had friends (Peter and Susie) with whom we often socialized—that is until a specific event occurred. After that, my husband refused dinner invitations with them. It seems that my husband did not appreciate the Christmas Day gift that Peter brought—a small truckload of horse manure. (We lived in the country, and I had a small garden.) But the final straw was Peter's compulsive talking about his wife's sexual behavior and about his "strained" finances (if they indeed were) at the dinner table. While Susie and I maintained a close relationship, it was no longer a foursome!

The avoidance of this social relationship certainly eliminated painful evenings for both of us and, I imagine, for Susie as well. And while this example seems extreme, it is not unusual to streamline social relationships so that it is no longer necessary to attend unpleasant events.

Emotional Traits

Our emotional makeup is behind the development of personality traits, which, in turn, guide our behavior. Some of these traits are especially useful and significant for the older person, as we are often compelled to face unwelcome situations. While for some of us these traits are innate, others can develop them with a little practice, and these will lighten the burdens that come (Morakitou and Efklides 2007, p. 89).

Resilience. Resilience is a chameleon of feelings. This characteristic, above all, is important for us as we age. Resilience is how quickly or slowly we recover from emotions, especially the negative ones. It is the ability to change attitudes, feelings, and behavior to blend in positively with the situation. It is the ability to recover quickly from a disturbing event. Can we easily let go of anxiety-loaded situations over which we have no control? Or do we lie awake at night, unable to relax and sleep? Some people hold on to fears or grudges for years; some can let them pass after only an hour or a day.

Getting over it means the anger or hurt does not stick or intrude into other activities. For instance, an angry disagreement does not carry over to the next activity. Or a difficult day at work does not affect the feelings upon arriving home. Resilient persons usually do not have their sleep disturbed by worry, realizing the problem is better handled in the morning.

Physical, familial, and social situations are increasingly more difficult to control as life brings unexpected demands. Resilience is that inner elasticity that wraps around a new situation like a rubber band. Not changing it but molding to it. For instance, many older persons experience time in a hospital setting in which they must fit in with the rules and expectations of others. Resilience refers to melding with that situation and accepting its demands so that the greatest health, comfort, and contentment can be maintained.

A lack of resilience is a self-defeating attitude. One patient, a forty-five-year-old woman, was angry that a statue of a Greek goddess, owned by her father, had been claimed by her sister upon their father's death. She had received a fair share from the inheritance, but that one statue, that one thing, became the symbol of the lifelong competition between them. She could not forgive her sister for taking it. Two years later, she and her sister had not yet spoken. She had little resilience and little acceptance of the situation. And she had lost her relationship with her sister, for a statue.

As we age, we face many new and unanticipated situations, with increasingly less control over events. It becomes increasingly important that we relax, that we accept new situations, and that we focus on the pleasant aspects of life.

Emotional responsiveness to the complexity of everyday life becomes softened. Our understanding and the meaningfulness of once disturbing situations lessen any need to react. This ability to regulate emotional expressions brings a decrease in the frequency, duration, and intensity of emotional reactions. For instance, older couples often ignore an action or statement of the partner that once might have initiated an angry rebuttal or a heated argument. A patient, Ned, was a compulsive talker, but his wife had only to give him a meaningful look or a toss of her head, and he would end his monologue. It was a subtle gesture, brought on by intimacy and comfort with each other.

Optimism. Optimism is an important quality that contributes to a person's welfare. It is the ability to see the glass half-full rather than half-empty. This attention to the positive and the pleasant aspects of life, perhaps naively seeing the world through rose-colored glasses, even when it seems difficult, opens a situation to pleasant possibilities. A positive outlook tends to make difficult situations easier and keeps hope alive. This quality helps to ensure a longer life.

Others see the dark side and respond to a negative interpretation of the situation. Harboring this pessimistic outlook, they expectl that the worst may happen. The pessimistic outlook is based on fears of previous disappointments. As such, it is a trait that guards against further disappointment in life, but a result is that a negative attitude will increase anxiousness as well as the ability to resolve problems. And indeed, pleasure is robbed from life.

Anxiety. Some are driven by possible mishaps, fears and feelings. They tend to overreact to many situations—stressful events or even joyous occasions. These anxious persons are fearful of changes and of new or unknown situations. Change is particularly difficult for them; their world becomes unpredictable, and a sense of safety is lost. As stresses of aging increase with illness, change of residence, and/or loss through death of a person close to them, anxiousness increases (Daatland 2013, p. 372). These tense persons embrace little inner calm. Sadly, the anxiousness often increases with age.

Disgruntlement. When we run into a grumpy old character, they were like that before growing old. They were grumpy then too. The "grumpy" remains, unconnected to the aging process. Chronically grouchy, the disgruntled person pushes feelings away with grumbles. It is a safe, self-protective facade. Curiously, while the tendency may be to ignore that person, grouchiness also serves to get them what they want. The disgruntled person uses the sour grapes approach or pessimistic attitude to ward off possible denials of affection and other feelings. Their tendency is to pull away or refuse to deal with emotionally loaded events. Sullenness or grouchiness conceals anxiety. And as with anxiousness, the grouchiness tends to increase with age—as stress increases. These apparently unhappy persons hide their fears, sadness, and loss of control over situations by pushing people away with being grouchy. Often it is an attempt to escape becoming lost in a depressive withdrawal from life.

Self-awareness. Improving the quality of emotional life often depends on our self-awareness. Is attention given to the emotional signals within ourselves? Do we pay attention to our reaction to ourselves? To others? To the event? Do we step closer or take a backward step from a person? Our *feeling* reaction is almost immediate. How we react *emotionally* to the signals our body gives is our choice.

I had an unusual experience talking to a young colleague. While he was talking, my face felt frozen; I could hardly speak. It was fear. I later found that he was extremely angry that I had been given a task that he had wanted. While he was controlling some hostility and aggression, I was struck with fear, as if attacked. Awareness of our own signals makes any situation more manageable as we recognize them. A better response can follow.

Emotional Expression as We Age

Emotions serve an essential role in coping with the challenges and help both our survival and sense of well-being, even when aging brings unusual stresses. All the evidence suggests that as we age, we gain an increased understanding of life. The acceptance and understanding eases stressful situations that might have overwhelmed us earlier in life. They help us now. As a consequence, aging can bring with it a more satisfying emotional life, more companionable friends, and a greater sense of contentment.

Over the last thirty to one hundred years, several universities and national organizations have been carrying out continuous studies of the effects of aging. The following summarizes the research on the emotional life of older persons.

First, as we grow older, many have fewer negative feelings, such as loneliness, depression, anger, and boredom. The sense of contentment seems to continue until the time that declining health issues set in and may result in depression or loneliness (Urry and Gross 2010).

Next, we will probably find that we are better able to regulate emotional reactions. We have gained greater control of when, where, and how we express our feelings, resulting from the various experiences we have had. The control over feelings lets us select more effective reactions and lessens our experience of aversive feelings, such as sadness, anger, and fear (Carstensen 2003).

We find that our social relationships become restricted to smaller but a more emotionally satisfying group of friends. This decreases unpleasant interactions and increases the sense of well-being (Carstensen 2003).

We now give more attention to positive rather than negative information (Isaacowitz et al.). It seems we tend to avoid negative stimuli, even in such a simple task as looking at pictures or watching television and/or movies. This research is interesting, for while presenting pictures to younger and older adults, older persons quickly shift their gaze from gruesome pictures to more pleasing ones.

We become better able to predict how we might feel in a stressful situation (Urry and Gross 2010). Consequently, we, as older adults, often choose not to engage in troublesome events because we know how the situation will make us feel.

We will probably experience higher levels of hedonic well-being until very late in life. This has been a consistent finding through many research projects and throughout the Western world. This means that we can expect to be more content and satisfied.

One last look at reality. There are two personality styles that show little peace as they age. Those who are anxiety-ridden persons and those who are grouchy, disgruntled persons do not seem to attain feelings of contentment. The stresses of aging overwhelm them, making it even more unlikely for them to alter their needs or their attitude toward life.

Severe stresses still provoke strong emotional reactions. We do not lose our feelings as we age.

It was Goethe who wrote, "If feeling fails you, vain will be your course."

And a pleasant surprise is that we found that pleasure and contentment increase for most people as they grow older. With increasing emotional competence, we can organize our lives to maximize positive feelings and minimize negative feelings. Maturity and life experiences have resulted in our ability to have greater control and regulation of emotional reactions.

With the complexity of everyday life, emotional responsiveness becomes modulated and softened as our understanding or meaningfulness of once disturbing situations changes the emotional reactions. This ability to regulate emotional expressions brings a decrease in the frequency, duration, and intensity of emotional reactions. Thus, life experiences bring an improvement in the sense of emotional well-being and emotional functioning. A sense of contentment, mellowness, and satisfaction increases.

Emotions serve an essential role in coping with the challenges of life and help both our sense of well-being and survival, even when the challenges increase in number and severity and the control over life is gradually diminished. In effect, all the evidence suggests that as we age, our experiences are usually directed toward an increased understanding of life that eases stressful situations. Therefore, age brings with it a more satisfying personal life, more companionable friends, and a greater sense of contentment.

Aging offers a unique opportunity. A different perspective on life is available as we become better acquainted with our inner selves. There is now freedom to know ourselves as never before, to permit a more honest inner perspective for and about ourselves. Time is there to use as we choose, to explore new challenges, and to explore new social relations. Devoid of the social roles that were worn before, we have a surprising opportunity to direct attention to the self. Enjoy it.

Chapter 8

Capture Those Fears

What are fears but voices airy?
Whispering harm where harm is not.
—Wordsworth

To deny the power of fear as "voices airy" is to deny the prisoner of a terror that fear brings. We know more fear than we did when we were younger because there are now more reasons for fear. We do not walk as rhythmically; it is more difficult to step onto or off a curb; our changing perception makes parking a car a more difficult task, and so on. We learn to be cautious whenever these situations arise.

Marvin, aged seventy-eight, lived alone. The thought of an intruder frightened him, giving him a dry mouth and anger. No one could ever come into his house unbidden. He placed three separate locks on each door to deter possible break-ins, although he lived in a very safe neighborhood.

Emma, aged seventy-nine, refuses invitations for dinner with friends; she no longer wants to drive at night. Before, social situations had been the high spots of her life; now her heart beats fast at the idea of leaving home alone.

Jack, aged seventy-five, could not attend his grandson's graduation, fearful of traveling, although during his professional life he traveled widely.

Faith, aged seventy-eight, was scheduled for a breast biopsy in the next week. She was overwhelmed with fears, trembling at the thought of surgery.

Maria, aged eighty-four, was fearful of staying alone for an hour while her husband attended a meeting nearby. They lived in an apartment in a senior residential center—in essence, the safest of environments. She was fearful that she might get ill and die when alone.

These persons were coping with their fears. Marvin is a good example of *primary* control; to alleviate his fear, he himself placed three additional locks on his doors. He was able to cope; he changed his environment to fit his needs.

Emma had cataracts and could not drive at night After her vision was restored, she remained fearful of night driving. She was successfully coping with the fear by using a *secondary* control mechanism—avoiding the situation. In essence, she gave up much of her social life unless a friend would escort her.

Jack had a panic attack on an airplane and did not want to fly again. His experience had been traumatic, and although attending his grandson's graduation was important to him—and his grandson—he chose a *secondary* coping behavior for himself—by not placing himself in the frightful situation. While avoidance alleviated his fears, it also robbed him of great pleasure. He was penned up at home, not attempting to travel necessary distances to visit family members.

Faith, aged seventy-eight, was scheduled for a breast biopsy. She was very anxious and apprehensive about the procedure, seeking consolation from friends. She relieved her anxiety by praying each night until the appointed day. She also used a *secondary* coping skill; she dealt with her anxiety through prayer, which provided her inner calm, believing that whatever the outcome, it would be "the Lord's will." It was an effective means for her to achieve some inner calm about the oncoming surgery.

Maria had a heart problem and a dread of dying alone. A neighbor had died alone, and it was two days before she was found. She used *primary* control in taking herself to the meetings in her wheelchair and secondary control in calming her fears by being present with others. This illustrates the interaction between primary and secondary control.

As fears persist, we may say, "I just don't feel like it," or "It is not important." Statements like those are logical, cautious, and reasonable, and they are self-protective. We don't like to say, "I am fearful," or "I am scared." As our lifestyle gradually changes, we "just don't do that anymore." Acknowledging the fear would make us face them.

Fear is a normal reaction to anything that threatens. It is a self-protective response, and thus we give attention to our fears. As we age, old fears are resurrected, and new fears come. Situations we once handled with ease and grace now may be frightening. The feelings may surprise us with their intensity. Fears become the parent of cruelty—robbing us of peace of mind. We are conscious of our loss of strength, impending vulnerability, and loss of self-confidence. What we once did, we do no more.

Fear is a powerful emotion. We have an example that will refresh the terror that fear can bring. Take time to think about walking in your backyard. Looking down at the ground, we see there is a snake writhing along the pathway. What happens? We scream, pull our bodies back away from it, throw our hands in the air, think of running, or we stand there paralyzed, unable to move. Fear can paralyze the ability to think, make choices, react to a situation, and even feel. Our heart beats faster, our breathing is difficult, our bodies quiver, and our vision and hearing are more alert. We cower and shake with thoughts of the feared.

Fear may cause us to resist or to deny or to freeze without the ability to do anything. We want to avoid the situation, and then if that is not possible, deny it. For instance, a suggestion such as "Dad, your hearing is not good; you need a hearing aid" garners the response "No, I don't. I hear all right." Losing one's hearing is something Dad does not want to know. So he pulls back and does not want to think or talk about it. This is a *flight* away from knowing the fear.

When the topic is later resumed, his response may be "I don't need a hearing aid. I hear all right if you don't mumble." When the fear is more imminent, we *fight* against it. We don't want to give in. An angry or stubborn response comes out. "I'll never use a hearing aid"—and yet that time may come.

When the threat is not to be avoided and our fear becomes intense, we may *freeze*. Our feelings are dulled. It is giving in to the inescapable—and acceptance of it.

Like the rabbit freezes when the fox is about to devour it; the rabbit has stopped trying to flee, becoming immobile to avoid being caught by becoming a stationary object.

I remember freezing as I was taken into the hospital for surgery. Like a rabbit that freezes when being chased by a fox, I was a robot. My feelings were dulled. I felt like an automaton. I moved mechanically, following the nurse. I had accepted the need for surgery but was fraught with fears so great I could not feel.

"Fear itself is not a foe but acquiescing to fear empowers it to be a formidable one."[xiv] It can dampen the spirit, make one cling to the known, compel one to run, or provoke anger. Fear is a natural protection against a threatening, new, or unexpected situation. Let us look at some fears that are foremost for aging people.

Fear and Anxiety

Change is a realistic aspect of life. In youth, changes are exciting and adventurous. In youth, we seek out new experiences. Even now, we enjoy the change of seasons, variations in the weather, and a ride in the country. The changes we see in the success of our children and in the growth of our grandchildren are delights. As we age, however, many changes bring a sense of loss of control over life and living. There are personal changes, physical changes, changes in our social lives, and often enough, changes in our economic status. And now the technological changes that are altering our lives make the world seem a strange place, sometimes enlarging the gap between generations.

The fears identified by seniors most frequently are as follows:[xv]

Losing independence. The fear of losing independence is greater and more terrifying than the fear of dying itself. We want to keep ourselves intact, to be independent and not to be helpless. The very thought strikes fear and even dread for most of us. We shun the thought of dependency; it brings fears of being unable to take care of ourselves. We want to keep our pride.

Our need to get around in the environment is important. To be able to come and go as we wish represents freedom. My mother, aged ninety-two, would drive one mile to get some ice cream—it gave her a sense of freedom (and ice cream *is* good!). She kept her driver's license until the end, although the last six months she was confined to bed. Giving up driving, for her and many others, can be traumatic; it is difficult to accept.

Yet other things infringe upon our freedom of moving about. Walking with a cane or a walker is a loss of freedom of movement; the need for glasses or hearing aids brings a loss of some autonomy. I know this well, for my loss of hearing made it impossible to talk on the telephone. Many an older person has refused to wear glasses or have a hearing aid—even when they would make life easier.

Health problems. Physical changes in our bodies appear uninvited. Yes, and even in healthy moments, we anticipate the possibility of illness or disability. Do physical changes or health problems bring fear? They did for me. For eight years, I could not hear; I was deaf. I feared isolation from friends and family, from people. I wondered how I would manage to be present with people without the ability to hear and talk with them. After all, I had been a psychotherapist, a profession that depends on hearing and on relationships with others. It was awful to think of a future without hearing. It was scary. I could not hear the doorbell, talk on the telephone, or enjoy social activities. (I was fortunate; a cochlear implant restored my hearing.)

Other, more serious health problems come as we grow older. Older people develop chronic illnesses—diabetes, heart problems, lung problems, and dementias are most common. All of them invite their own kinds of fear.

Fear of falling. Many of us have had a friend or relative who has fallen. The person may have slipped while walking or felt dizzy when standing up from a chair. Maybe you have fallen yourself; I have. I was lucky—no broken bones or concussions. Each year, at least 1.6 million older US adults go to emergency departments for fall-related injuries; more than one in three people aged sixty-five years or older falls each year.[xvi] And these falls often have severe repercussions. One friend, aged eighty-two, fell on her back in her home. She did not have a safety monitor or even a telephone handy. Finally, she was able to push herself on her back to the phone. The fall resulted in back surgery that thankfully was successful so that, after some rehabilitation therapy, she was able to walk again—but not with the ease of walking she had before the fall. This is just one of many stories we could all add.

Oftentimes a walk of any distance must be taken carefully, even fearfully, for, with age, our grace of movement disappears. We learn to watch each step, to hold on to the railing on the stairway, to watch the height of curbs. We walk more fearfully, more aware of each step. Safety demands the use of canes or walkers when helpful. Practical measures of safety include exercising to improve balance, removing loose rugs, adding handrails to stairways, and having good light in dark spaces.

Cognitive difficulties. In our present culture, the fear of the loss of our mental abilities is among the most feared health issues. It comes earlier in life than we like when we first recognize that some memory difficulties normally appear. It is embarrassing when, introducing a friend, we forget his/her name! Or walking into a room to find something and then forgetting what was wanted. These are common experiences as short-term memory loss challenges us. Often, they bring a smile to us or a good laugh with a friend.

But the fear of losing one's thinking and memory abilities provokes fear of dementia. When we ponder the loss of the ability to think or to solve problems, the loss of memory, or the loss of the sense of where we are or who our family members are, it is really frightening. Dementias of different causes seem to be increasing—or so it seems as we live longer. We will not discuss this because more information is available in many places. I suggest the National Institutes of Health on the internet as a good starting place for information. For our purposes in this book, we recognize this as a tremendous emotional challenge, for it is a strong, latent fear lying in our consciousness, only to become activated when the real possibility looms before us.

Fears of vulnerability. These fears come about as we lose our strength, vigor, and ability to take care of ourselves. These are fears of being attacked, of being robbed, and of walking alone. Marvin, in an opening illustration, felt very vulnerable, fearful of someone breaking into his home. He installed not one but three locks on his door. And I wonder if, even then, he had completely alleviated his anxiety.

Going out alone at night, driving a long distance, or trusting strangers are common potential fears. It is important that we meet them by providing for ourselves the safest environment possible.

Family well-being and illness. We remain concerned for our families, especially if there is an illness or other problems. Concerns about their health, their resources, and their well-being are manifestations of the bonds of love and care that we have for them—both for the present and for the future. We wonder about their future well-being as we watch our country struggle through environmental, social, international, and financial changes and difficulties. There is little that we can do about these huge problems, although we can discuss concerns and worries with our family. Perhaps there are suggestions we can provide to help in their planning for their future.

Death of family members and/or friends. Deaths of others we love are especially difficult to deal with. The longer we live, the more familiar we become with dying and death. The loss of yet another person deepens the sadness and grief that other deaths have brought. Each death presents a crisis; each is a trauma. And with it, we acknowledge anxiety about our own death.

The death of a special person makes the recognition of our own approaching death nearer. We live with a memory of them fresh within us; we live with them in recognizing the part of ourselves they filled. We know better the contributions they made to our life. We become more aware of the preciousness of each day, of memories we may leave behind us, and of feelings of love and tenderness toward those in our daily life.

Changes of residence. The necessity of changing our place of residence is frightening. Perhaps our home now requires too much care, or we are too disabled to stay there, or we live too far from our children. Living in a child's home or with a relative seems like a great loss of freedom. It is being dependent, living under their roof, with their rules, habits, and style of living. One is no longer with familiar objects or in control.

Moving to a senior citizen residence is also strange—a big change with the loss of home, neighborhood, and friends. At first, it may seem like an impersonal environment—a hotel. The fears flow away as we meld into the environment, meet others who share some of our circumstances, and find new friendships. It becomes our place, our home.

Almost no one wants to be so ill that we spend our last days in an impersonal environment, dependent on the care of strangers and away from family and friends. But one conflict that we deal with is that we do not want to be a burden to family or friends. Yet in our heart of hearts, most of us would prefer to be taken care of by family or friends—or at least by those professionals we choose. We do not want to place a burden on anyone, to have them caring for us, yet we do not want the separation from them or the lostness that a nursing home or hospice suggests. The thought that a stranger will prepare food, bathe, or help us dress feels embarrassing, lonely, scary, or dreadful. We question, *What will I be like? How ill will I be?*

As older age comes upon us, we know that death awaits all. I only hope to die quietly, with a sense of gratitude for all the goodness given me during life. Even though there is little possibility that I, or most people, can know when or where or how we will die, thoughts as these prepare us—yet do not really allay the fear.

Finances. The fear of a lack of money and resources is a major concern. It affects most of us. About one half of us are living solely on Social

Security and Medicare; this is living below the poverty line. An inner terror arises, as we could be forced to choose between essential items such as food and medicine. Sometimes, relatives may help. Thankfully, some state and national programs can provide some help—and could be investigated before they are necessary—if that is possible.

Fearing the loss of self. All these fears can be summed up in the greatest fear of all: the loss of the sense of self, the loss of realizing who we are and who our family members are. Other fears fade into nothing in comparison. To be a person, to make choices, to feel, and to communicate with others are first in importance even unto death.

Relieving Fears: Feeling Better

The emotional challenge of aging is to change the fears into a deeper knowledge of oneself. Each fearful situation can be met and allayed. Fear can be lessened, and anxieties resolved by confronting the challenges that face us. One approach is utilization of the selectivity-optimization-compensation problem-solving method:

First, acknowledge the fear or anxiety about the situation. Say, "I am anxious about or afraid of ..."

I am afraid of moving to a senior citizen residence. I really don't want to move.

Now think about the situation in detail. What makes me afraid? What about the situation brings the fear? Try to pinpoint the fear.

I won't know anybody there. I may not be able to keep busy the way I am at home. I will be lonely.

Now, picture the situation. What do you see?

Will I meet anybody? Will they like me? What will I do with all my time?

Now hold onto those thoughts and mental images as a guide for the next step.

It is a big place. I won't know how to find anything. I see myself wandering around empty halls, not even finding the dining room or getting back to my own apartment. The dining room is big; it is very attractive with white tablecloths. The food seemed pretty good too. It may not be that scary, because there a lot of people there.

Let the thoughts and images give way to curiosity about the change. Ask yourself: What will it be like? How can I manage it? What can I do?

What will it feel like? How can I help myself feel better? What will the others be like and how will I feel about them?

It will be strange not knowing where to go. Perhaps I can write down the number of the apartment, so I at least know where I live. I can ask someone how to get to the dining room. Perhaps they will provide a map of the community so I can use that. I can carry my phone and ask the desk where things are. It will be scary at first. I may get confused, but I will get used to it.

It might be fun to meet new people. Most of my friends are gone anyhow. I wonder how the other people are—friendly or scared too. Maybe I can even find a lonely man to eat with or play cards or accompany to activities. That would be nice. Or maybe meet some nice women friends. With all those people there, I can find new friends. I wonder if my clothes will be all right.

Curiosity makes for some flexibility as possible choices are anticipated and responses to possible difficulties are formed. The preparation opens a path to new choices. Plan about choice, even actions.

And then consider what you will need or want to make up any lacks in the new situation: compensation.

There are not many books there; perhaps I should buy a Kindle so that I have more books available, or I can order books on Amazon. That is a good idea. I can even order movies for myself.

While this approach seems simple and all too easy, it is a straightforward preparation for change and alleviates fears and anxieties. It provides an opportunity to vicariously run through possible difficulties and makes us mentally familiar with situations. It is an active appraisal of the feared situation that lets us restructure the problem. It modulates the fear and gives more control.

It is well established that older persons can select the best choice for themselves, select the situation that is best in their feelings, identify drawbacks to their choices, and then plan compensation for them.

Rational, everyday fears are there to protect us. We remain careful when crossing the street, walking up and down the stairs, avoiding fires, and so on. Our feelings are to be honored, to be used for our safety.

But when fears intrude into daily life, when fears despoil a situation, anxiety rules the spirit. To be infested with fear is a cruelty. Fears can become tyrants that kill the spirit. Perhaps the most powerful response to our fears and anxieties comes with preparation for each situation. Let yourself know the change. Inner contentment and peace will come with the insight into and understanding of the fearful situation.

Chapter 9

The Emotional Challenge of Loneliness

Woe to him that is alone! For if he falleth, there is none to pick him up.
—Ecclesiastes 4:10

We have all had moments of being alone. Sometimes it is a welcome relief after a busy social day. Sometimes it is the pleasure of walking alone in the park. Sometimes it is the glory of solitude. Sometimes it is the loneliness of the soul, a deep sense of desolation. Being alone is often our plight as we age. We sorrow about the loss of partners, family, and friends. Let us now explore the experiences of being alone and how being alone may affect us.

Aloneness, solitude, isolation, and loneliness all apply to being without others—in spirit or reality. Without others near—the quietness, the need for it, the peacefulness of it, the sadness of it, the pain, the desolation, and the isolation- all refer to the absence of others. Being alone is a major emotional challenge for us as we age.

More than 43 percent of people over seventy say they are lonely, although only 18 percent live alone.[xvii] Being lonely impairs health. In loneliness, our immune system is under stress; that means the lonely person is more likely to develop colds and infections, and existing illnesses may worsen. This study also reported that the persistence of feeling lonely was a predictor of the decline of functioning and of earlier death.

Aloneness is a time when we are on our own. Either by choice or happenstance, being alone often provides a time when there is no need for someone. Many of us seek time to be alone, to do what we wish, to think;

it brings a sense of relief from expectations of others. We love the quietness when guests leave and we are alone in our home.

Solitude requires aloneness. It is being alone without being lonely. It is a desirable time in which you provide yourself wonderful and sufficient company. It is a time of refreshment of the spirit and of opportunity to renew ourselves. It is a time of reflection. Solitude is enjoying the quietness and brings peacefulness within oneself. We cherish and seek these times. The older person who enjoys solitude is to be envied, for he/she enjoys the richness of their own being.

Isolation is the aloneness we find when someone is cut off from people. When it is by choice, it suggests a seclusion that has been sought by someone—to be alone, to find quietness, to work. On the other hand, many an isolated older person has not chosen it; circumstances have left them alone. They may be desolate with their isolation.

Loneliness mars the life of many an older person. It is to feel terrible, awful; there is no one to be with you. Loneliness is a sense of desperation, of having lost contact with others and with oneself. It is painful distress. And it is a problem that descends on many. Lonely people have no meaningful contact with others. There is no confidante. They talk with none on a personal, intimate level and have none to share their feelings or to share closeness and intimacy. The deaths of spouses and friends have left them abandoned; those persons dear to us are difficult to replace. New friends rarely fill that empty spot in the hearts of lonely people.

The Need for Relationships

There are three basic psychological needs. First, a sense of *autonomy*—that is a sense of control over one's behavior and situation. Then a sense of *competence*—that is to feel effective in our actions. And third, a sense of *relatedness* to others. Of the three psychological needs, the primary emotional need is relatedness to others; it is feeling connected to others and belonging to a social group. For without relatedness, there comes diminished physical vitality, loss of desire to do anything, and a loss of well-being. Depression may set in. Each moment becomes tiresome; it seems time has stopped.

During the years of growing, there is an increase of numbers in the friendship circle. As we reach adulthood, we became engaged with an increasing number of people—family, friends at school, colleagues at work, neighbors, organizations. To the contrary, aging brings about a reversal of the number and frequency of contact with others. This is a normal reduction in the frequency of social relationships and interactions. Retirement, change of residence, loss of participation in organizations, and loss of friends and family through death gradually decrease the number of social contacts. The circle returns to the beginning, and we are then alone again. Loneliness may well be a first feeling for the baby. It is often the last feeling experienced by the aging and dying person.

Many interactions with others have focused on superficial and impersonal talk, such as at work. As one withdraws from many daily activities that involved others, there are fewer reasons to maintain contact with all these people. We become increasingly selective in relationships and prefer to spend time with those whose company is gratifying and pleasing. These relationships continue to affirm our self-concept, make us feel better, and in general are the most emotionally rewarding of social relationships. These relationships are warm or fun or may simply provide time to share memories and to engage in mutually preferred activities.

A factor that I would like to overlook but cannot, is age discrimination—that is, being socially rejected because of being older. Just looking older—as becoming grayer, more wrinkled, more bent—is enough to shorten relationships with some people or organizations. Often the committee, workplace, or organization wants a "fresh" look—someone new and younger. Also, some people shy away from those who are older. Until recently, age itself has been sufficient to limit participation in working situations or organizations. Gradually, this discrimination is decreasing because of new laws, but it does not change personal attitudes toward the aged.

My mother had a distressing experience in her church. She was a member of a sewing circle that met once a month to make supplies such as quilts and blankets for the local charities. She had been a member of this group for many years. An expert in sewing, she had contributed much, but one day she was given a nonsense task by their new, young leader, who let her know that she was too old to be part of the sewing group. This type of subtle and not-so-subtle fear or dislike of older persons is active, although not stated aloud—even among well-meaning people. Since volunteerism is a major pastime for senior citizens, the underlying message is that there is a time when one becomes too old even for volunteering.

Aloneness: The Emotional Challenge

There are three different kinds of aloneness. There is solitude or seclusion, unwanted loneliness, and the lonely person. First, there are those who prefer seclusion and isolation. They are often engaged in activities that are solitary—such as writing, painting, sewing, or gardening. These persons do not experience much need for social relationships. They often choose to avoid involvement in groups or organizations; they have a few friends and prefer the intimacy they offer. Einstein said, "The monotony and solitude of a quiet life stimulate the creative mind." This is their creed.

Sometimes the seclusion is the result of having experienced emotional abuse from others. One patient I know had been emotionally abused as a child, leaving her with a fear of people and low self-esteem. Then in marriage, she was emotionally and physically abused by her husband. After thirty years of marriage, she chose to live alone—without friends—only relating to those whom she saw in actions of living, as clerks in the grocery store, medical personnel, and so on. She was an attractive, educated, and even pleasant person, but she could no longer trust or have confidence in others who might have offered friendship or intimacy. She was not bitter; she loved music and claimed it as her solace. She chose social isolation.

The second kind of loneliness, the unwanted loneliness that we meet, is found in those people who have always been lonely. This loneliness is internal. It is a deep, almost irremediable loneliness. Usually, they endured a childhood of being alone, of being friendless, unloved, and helpless to change it. They go through life alone, unable to find or accept the closeness of friends. They retain loneliness as a dominating mood. These persons are unhappy, and by their fifties, they have higher blood pressure, react more strongly to stress, and often end up in severe depression, even suicide.[xviii]

One patient, Susan, a fifty-year-old attorney, had no friends, although she yearned for them. She reported that she had never had friends, even as a child. When meeting a new possible friend, she overwhelmed them with gifts and invitations to join her in activities, and she sought to spend every free minute with them. The friendship would last a short time, maybe even a month. Then Susan would be rebuffed, as the "friend" could not tolerate Susan's neediness for constant company. She became lonelier than ever, felt unlovable, and eventually committed suicide.

Her story? Susan was an unwanted child of an older mother. When I interviewed her mother, she told me that she had not held Susan until she was about nine months of age. Her parents were alcoholic socialites. Susan was lonely at home and in school. At no time in her life, not even as a successful professional, could she have a positive sense of herself as a worthy individual. She endured deep loneliness that led to increased depression and resulted in her suicide at age fifty-three. This is *not* the loneliness that besets aging people.

When loneliness besets older people, it usually follows the experience of the gradual loss of relationships with family and friends; this is referred to as *external loneliness*. When we lose our connections with others, we are alone. Affection, intimacy, and warmth disappear from our lives. We may be inconsolable and grief-stricken. We feel lost, removed from others, and unable to reach out to others.

With older persons, when loneliness is chronic or becomes complicated with grief, depression may set in. Health problems are multiplied. It is well documented that health problems may develop through the effects of constant loneliness.[xix] Loneliness increases the stress of daily living, and each day seems dark and gloomy. The physical cost includes an increase in cardiovascular disease and stroke, a decrease in memory and learning skills, poor decision-making, and alcoholism.

Marcia, sixty-five years of age, had been a very socially oriented person. After her husband died, she withdrew into her home. With his loss, her plans and hopes for the future were gone. She lost contact with her friends partly because she was convinced that couples often avoid the newly singled person. The next ten years found her disinterested in earlier interests, such as music and painting. She lost any sense of purpose in her life and felt everything was futile, and as could be predicted, her loneliness was complicated by depression. Then something happened to her that rarely occurs. She was in an accident and severely injured. This trauma, along with the care of doctors and nurses, snapped her out of depression, and she began to resume a more normal life. She began to paint again, started volunteering in community activities, and regained a zest for life. For her, the gift of renewed life renewed her interest in life.

Perhaps the worst picture of desolateness and disconsolateness is seen in nursing homes or hospices. Here, there are often devoted nurses and other staff who care tenderly for the dying persons. They provide continuously and patiently for the needs and desires of the patients. Yet people sit, often dissociated and seemingly unaware of themselves and their environment, heads down, alone, looking at nothing, doing nothing. It is one of the saddest sights to behold. Most of them, when you speak with them, respond to social stimulation.

We do not choose that desolation. As I picture the desolation of this setting, there is a feeling of hurt deep in my soul.

Conquering Loneliness

Loneliness eats at the soul. It is a feeling of no one there, and it robs one's energy; it is an overwhelming sadness. To dispel loneliness demands more effort on the part of the older person, even though one's psychological and physical resources are limited. Given the fact that many older persons are alone and feel alone, they are now compelled to take more charge of their lives than ever before. To dispel loneliness takes action to seek a friend or group. And physical activity is most important for sparkling up one's mood and thinking.

It is imperative that we take responsibility for ourselves and our feelings. The following are simple suggestions. Any activity helps, and some ideas will appeal more than others.

- Keep a calendar of what you will be doing this week; write it down.
- First on the list should be a walk. Exercise is a necessity. Movement stimulates the body and mind in a positive manner. If you cannot walk, exercise the muscles that you can. See a physical therapist or your medical doctor for suggestions. Exercise provides the body with stimulation, increases energy, and energizes a sense of well-being.
- Every evening, plan for the tomorrow. Write it down, even if it is just planning what to wear or eat for breakfast.
- Make a list of things to do. Include small actions, like a smile at a passing stranger or saying hello to someone you do not know. You will be surprised at how often others return the smile. Practice smiling at others. Smiling lifts the spirit. Go to the grocery store, buy a new shirt, walk about the mall with a cart. Just going out of the house helps. Talk to your neighbors. Recognize that others may feel more awkward or shy than you—reach out and take the initiative.

- If you have interests in activities that are nonsocial, such as reading, sewing, working puzzles, painting, or using an iPad, do them. These activities help elevate the mood and lessen the anxiety that comes with loneliness.
- Attend church or other social groups—even if you are shy.
- Keep a journal of your favorite memories with your spouse or children—this is invaluable for them, and they will love it. Just writing one memory a day is good. For instance, my mother wrote in her recipe book, "I loved making this bread for you all." Forty years later, I keep that page!
- What would you be interested in seeing, doing, or knowing before life is gone? Make a list. Whom would you like to contact again? Plan how you could do it.
- Join a class for meditation. This will provide a look at your inner self and give you the courage to try new things. And it has been shown as effective in relieving the lostness of depression and loneliness.

Finally, and most importantly, plan an action that involves another. Begin with simple acts, such as determining to smile at the first three people you encounter; writing a card to a friend or relative; visiting a library or museum, go to a group meeting, or…

In these modern times, the technology of the computer brings the world to our homes. We can have Facebook friends, we can share information or stories, we can play interactive games, and we can even participate in email relationships. Of course, caution must be taken with these new machines.

Being alone can be a welcome time for contentment. Time alone can provide precious moments of viewing our life, of looking around, of noticing the little things.

Loneliness is different. Do not suffer from the loneliness in your spirit.

Chapter 10

Loves and Losses

I was fascinated and thrilled. Phil and Anna, an older couple, walked away from the church holding hands. When a teenager, this looked wonderful to me, to see that love and romance continued even into old age. I wanted a relationship like that. Even now, a similar sight brings warm feelings to me.

Love is a natural bond that holds people together. We seek the intimacy that brings joy when together and sadness when apart. We desire physical contact and physical presence with that person. We want to see, touch, and hear them. When he/she is absent, we feel alone and lost.

The love between parents and children forms character and the quality of relating to others. Then throughout life, we seek a love that parents *ideally* provided. That all-encompassing security, safety, and acceptance we idealize that parents give or should give—and later we seek this love in spouses and special friends. To a great degree, the emotional patterns of relating that we learn early in life stay with us. Often, they affect our choice of spouses and friends.

Families provide us with enduring relationships. As we grow older, we long to renew or restore family relationships even though we have been separated by time and distance. When feelings have been tainted and marred by unhappy memories, our heart carries the feelings for what could have been. We hope for a better relationship, and we hope to heal any hurt from the past, even if we have given up trying.

I have three brothers and three sisters. My attachment is different with each of them. I love each of them. I admired and respected my oldest brother, who was successful in life. I was more engaged with the next brother, who was closer in age, for he taught me many skills—such as how to change a spark plug and a flat tire on the car. My younger brother, I simply loved from the day he was born, and I still do. And so on, for each of my sisters. And they would describe their attachment to me in quite different ways.

Friendships provide us with love in a different way. When I was ten years old, I had a friend, Marjory. We giggled, ran around, and played together. Her family moved, and I lost touch with her. To this day, she is a friend I lost. I miss that special bond we shared. Childhood friendships are dear. When we meet childhood friends as adults, as at a reunion, what a great reconnection! We laugh at our childhood antics, woes, and competitions. All the escapades seem so unimportant when contrasted with how long the bond has endured. The bonds are intense within us, often remaining through our lives—at least in memories. These are old friends that share our memories of childhood.

Presently, thanks to the internet, I stay in contact with a high school friend. He was not a close friend, although we were both leaders in the class. I had not seen him for twenty-five years; we met at the high school reunion that year. Since then, and that was thirty years ago, we have remained in contact. We are both happily married; there is no romance. Our lives have been different, and our political convictions quite contrary. Yet we are having the most delightful give-and-take on issues of the day. We shall probably never meet. I value his friendship and communication. My feelings are warm and loving toward him and his wife. The internet has been, in this case, a welcome contribution to friendship.

Friendships in adulthood are especially important. They provide intimacy and support, recreation, and discussions. Mostly they bring pleasant emotional interactions. When we share *empathy* with another, that bond is special, that person, dearer. In many instances, friendship provides an intimacy that family members may not. And friendships are important for health. In these years of so much moving about, friendships grow more difficult to develop and keep. One study that followed the same persons throughout life for eighty years reported that persons with "great social networks were much more likely to live into their seventies, eighties and nineties" (Friedman and Martin 2011, p. 167).

Patterns of Attachment

As we realize, there are many kinds of love: mother-infant attachment, father-infant bond, sibling and familial bonds, friendship bonds, and sexual-pair bonds. Here, we are concerned with the bonds that affect us most as we age. The bond with a spouse is usually the most intimate and contributes most to emotional well-being.

The quality of relationships varies widely. The bond that we share with a spouse may be described within four patterns. The patterns are secure attachments, anxious-fearful attachments, anxious-ambivalent attachments, and anxious-dismissive attachments. There are other relationships that are more unstable, disorganized, confused, and emotionally colored that are not discussed herein.

Secure attachment. A secure attachment is characterized by trust, honesty, and a belief that one is worthy of love. Secure adults have a positive self-image and an expectation that others are accepting and responsive.

In the opening paragraph of this section, I talked about an elderly couple, Phil and Anna, holding hands while walking. What a pleasant picture this was. A couple who was touching, walking in step, and giving attention only to each other demonstrated a secure relationship.

Secure attachments are characterized by the following:[xx]

- Both feel safe when the other is nearby and responsive.
- Both value their close relationship but are not overly distraught when the other is inaccessible.
- With spouses, both engage in close, intimate bodily contact. Both trust and rely on the other; seek comfort from each other.
- Both are confident that the other will be there for them when needed.
- Both share feelings of warmth and love toward the other.

When the relationship is secure, joys, problem, and hopes are shared. Couples turn to each other for comfort and understanding; they expect acceptance and not judgment during difficult times. The secure attachment may also be experienced with family members and friends. It is easy to acknowledge that James and Jill had a secure relationship. Their marriage, their relationship, was strengthened through the crisis of illness. They were content to be together.

About 60 percent of married couples over sixty-five years of age report they have a secure relationship with their partners. They are content. I remember fondly the evening scene with my mother and father embracing each other. When I married, I expected this expression of love and warmth from my husband and received it.

There are a few relationships in which some difficulties have not occurred. When distress arises within a secure attachment, there is mutual support; they talk about and resolve it together and relieve the stress for both. With this confidence and support, storms are weathered. Safety and love are there.

The loss of a special person who has provided that secure love takes a drastic emotional toll. If a spouse or a parent dies, it may seem unbearable to have a life without the person. Even so, the grief is honest; the person's image may remain ever near.

Anxious-fearful attachments.[xxi] There are some people that are always insecure. They are anxiously fearful of the loss of love. They seek the reassurance of love; they need constant emotional support and closeness. Ridden with anxiety and insecurity, the neediness may seem cloying to the partner. Any stress makes them more emotionally needy and unsure of their partner's support. The bonds are as intense, but the love pattern is "Do you love me?" "Do you really love me?" "Do you really, really love me?" "Will you love me if …?"

These relationships are characterized by a concern that others do not reciprocate the desire for intimacy. Ambivalence and resistance to closeness are typical. It is a warm-cold existence, without trust.

Characteristics may include the following:

- negative self-image; positive image of the other
- a sense of unworthiness
- seek constant reassurances of love
- difficult in trusting and relying on their partner
- craves and needs intimacy

Example: Edna and Edward typify this kind of relationship. Edward had forgotten her fortieth birthday. After ten years of marriage, she could not be assured that he still loved her. Is she still lovable although forty years old? Her fears could not be assuaged. All her past fears of being abandoned, of being left on her own, were resurrected. And, of course, the more support she needed, the more Edward withdrew. He could not provide emotional support because he often feared a loss of autonomy. His defense was to deny, to stiffen himself against expressing how he felt. He often turned away from her cries. The more she needed, the less she received. For Edward could not accept her neediness. He too was dealing with stress and fears of losing her, but he could not let himself know them.

The sense of comfort and love when all is going smoothly brings a deep sense of togetherness that both have yearned for. Anxious couples seem to have more highs and lows in their relationships. They are at times exceptionally close and at other times distant from each other. Anxious persons scan the horizon for signs of impending rejection, seeing even relatively innocent events as posing a threat to the relationship.

Anxious-ambivalent attachment. This marital bond is an anxious, insecure relationship that leads to controlling and unpredictable relationships. Each needs to maintain a sense of independence and invulnerability.

The characteristics may be as follows:

- have a sometimes-positive view of themselves and a negative view of the partner
- want independence, and control in relationships
- distance themselves when pressured to give or receive support
- seek less comfort and support from partners; less likely to offer support to partner
- are less committed to relationships
- feel inadequate, unworthy
- hesitant to express or disclose feelings
- desire intimacy, yet fears of accepting closeness
- lack of trust in the partner

They are often blunt in speaking and say what they mean without sugarcoating. They have coping skills of invulnerability (you cannot hurt me) and belittle the need for others.

Bob and Jean had been married for fourteen years when I met them. Both were working as computer experts in the same company. They were well matched in many ways. Both were tall, attractive, athletic persons. Both loved sports, cinema, and many other activities, which they enjoyed together. When it came to intimacy and sexuality, they were matched in reverse. He was too fast; she, too slow. As a child, she had been sexually abused and needed a slow approach. He accused her of extramarital activities; *he* was the one who was unfaithful. These accusations and failure of empathy were the fuses for daily incidents of anger and accusations. She bore the blame for all inadequacy—whether sexual or something else.

When they made up, their life was heavenly for a week or two—never longer. They would not divorce because of the three children. Counseling did help, for they are still together and have grandchildren. They report that they are more content than before. There was no physical abuse between them, only emotional abuse.

The loss of a person in an anxious-ambivalent relationship brings a complexity of feelings. Emotional ties were confused and confusing—longing for love, disappointment, anger, sadness, and relief. The death of a partner stimulates a sense of guilt, longing, and mourning that is difficult to resolve. Thoughts such as "If only I ..." or "Why did he/she die just now?" serve to prolong the mourning and complicate the grieving. The bereaved person's grief may be difficult. Recovery from the loss is difficult because guilt often lingers, emotional gratification was inconstant, and anger, not assuaged. Their grief is often prolonged.

Anxious-dismissive attachments.[xxii] This kind of relationship occurs when a person desires/avoids the need for closeness and intimacy. It is a constant seeking to maintain independence yet is overly dependent on the partner. This cloak of over independence rises from deep inner fear and lack of trust that others could care for them. Roles are defined: he does this, and she does that.

Anxiety comes from deep fears of trust and safety. Intimacy is experienced as clinging, neediness, or feeling suffocated by the other person. In marriage, they want an ideal parent. At the same time, they are fearful of the feelings of dependency and insist on their own independence.

Some characteristics are as follows:

- ambivalent feelings about the self
- need for sense of independence and private space
- intimacy avoided except under conditions
- fears of trust and safety
- dependency on partner is easily denied
- feelings not consciously available; dull un-responsivity
- roles with partner defined by rules

Example: Charles's wife, Carla, became ill with cancer. She was given a prognosis of three months to live. During these three months, he instigated an affair with his secretary. He ignored, even ran, from the support his wife needed and from the love that she could give him. Her need, her illness, made him anxious. He denied and dismissed her need for support even during these predictable last days of her life.

Charles represents this anxious-dismissive style of bonding. At a time when feelings of love and possible loss surge within him, he pulls away and seeks another relationship. A new relationship becomes a defense against the sense of loss mounting within him. He remains dismissive of the importance of the relationship with his wife and seldom visits her. He seems to go about his own life without regard for his partner's illness.

Yet marriages like this may last. When the partner is of a giving, generous nature and there is no physical abuse, the distrust of the dismissive person can gradually be undone.

People can and do change. While the scars of insufficient love from childhood may provide a base of feelings toward others, experiences do alter earlier conditions. Especially when the person realizes for himself/herself that others provide different love that can alter learned patterns and more gratifying attachments can be attained.

Losses and Love

I met a friend for lunch. For two years, she was the caretaker for her ill father, who had died a month earlier. When she called, her voice was light and joyful. She seemed released from the captivity that caretaking sometimes feels like. She expressed that she had a restful month, traveling to see a friend—with no breakdown of grief. We had no more than spoken a few words together when she burst into tears. Her sorrow burst forth, no longer held back.

I am a friend of grief. I say this because I have experienced the deaths of many—including those nearest and dearest to me. I know, and at this age, *we* know that sorrow is a friend; the emotions of loss are part of us, of our life experience. I know, and we know, the shock of death, expected or not. We are seldom ready to have that person leave us. There is always a little unfinished sense, a little reason to want that person back, if just for a moment.

I know the pangs in the heart that grief brings. Pictures of the dying persons lingered in my mind; death is trauma. Sorrow and grief are the emotional paths to recovery after the loss. The inner emptiness that follows, the physical fatigue, the loss of interest, the need for aloneness all invade us. The support of friends helps—a little at first, more later. Gradually the images of sickness and death disappear; happier memories come.

Grief helps us heal. Grief brings the emotional release that helps us adapt to the absence of the person. A plethora of emotions come and go. Sadness, numbness, loneliness, anger, rage, self-reproach, anxiety, yearning, and relief all intermingle. Grief helps to recreate an emotional world that has fallen apart. The journey of grief is a voyage into darkness and sorrow. The pain of grief is a sign of love.

Sometimes the grief is complicated because of an anxious attachment to that person. To resolve conflicted love about a person who dies demands a reappraisal of the relationship, recreating an understanding look at the person, recognizing one's own contribution to any conflict, and, more importantly, assuming the responsibility for one's own actions and feelings in the relationship.

On the surface of a relationship marked by an avoidant-dismissive attachment, the mourning seems emotionally uninvolved. Emotional expressions are limited, although the words show the intensity of the loss. Feelings are tightly contained within, but when the lost closeness is realized and the emptiness of their soul breaks forth, they are inconsolable—a delayed grieving.

The gray of mourning colors the loss of spouse, family, and friends. Special persons in our lives who enrich our daily living are gone. Life changes. To cling to mourning, to nurture the sadness of loss is to undermine the joy the person brought. To cling to mourning minimizes the person's special importance. It belittles their love. To cling to mourning is to destroy the light of their life.

Know them more clearly now, even more honestly. Remember especially their goodness, their smile, and the special person they were. Let yourself know their humaneness, their humanity, their weakness; enjoy the gifts of pleasure they gave. Bask in it. Find peace by enshrouding their memory with joy. Letting go is an emotional challenge of aging.

Grieve loss but not death. Mourn love withheld but not love given.[xxiii]

Chapter 11

Loves and Losses, Part II: Homes and Possessions

My parents had lived in their home for about forty years when my father suddenly died. The next year brought many changes for my mother—leaving her home and neighborhood, moving into my sister's home, and giving up her furniture and other belongings. Only much later did I discover her great sorrow at leaving the old upright piano behind. I had never realized how much the piano had meant to her, at what great cost she had purchased it, and how much of her life's pride had been invested in providing each child with music lessons to enrich their life. She loved the piano, and as she said, in memory, she could hear us practice. (Oh! Good?)

This is a common experience; there are special things and objects, not especially in and of themselves but for what they represent—a moment of joy, a sign of love, a remembrance of an event. Is this so strange? These special things are invested with feelings and treasured for them.

When a baby cries and seems inconsolable, what does the parent do? The parent gives the child a symbol that comforts the baby. Whether it be a security blanket, teddy bear, or another thing, it provides solace. The crying stops. What is this connection to a thing that brings ease to the baby? How do things, even to the baby, become so significant, so important?

Attachment to things. We invest a lot of emotional energy in things that have accompanied an event of significance. For instance, I wear a ring that my husband gave me; I do not want to give it up. I wear it all the time even though he has been gone for twenty years. The ring renews the feeling of his love for me; I can feel his presence. Like the baby with a security blanket, the ring has become a part of me.

There are other things I cherish, such as a set of dishes my mother gave me when I married, pictures that my brother painted, and my desk that is fifty years old. We become attached to those things that represent parts of our life; they have become part of us, of our identity; they are filled with memories of love and warmth. It is almost as if we fear that when they are gone, the memories or feelings will dissipate. That is, of course, not true, for the feelings remain, even though they may be more easily activated by the presence of those things. It will be very difficult when I say goodbye to those things.

It is equally true that some symbols may be of difficult times or events—that the memory is filled with confusion or sad or angry feelings. These symbols, these things, are often easier to give up. Some things we are glad to be rid of. The objects were never emotionally important to us—although they may have been to someone else. We just may not like them.

Attachments to our home. Many are compelled to change residence when we grow older. The reasons are multiple: some want to live nearer to children; some want to live in a warmer climate; some may become too disabled to maintain their home; or some may want to live in a safer place, nearer medical care and other services.

Moving from one's home is a major stress for younger persons; it is traumatic for the older person. A home is a place of familiarity and security. It reflects the personality of the individual—the likes and dislikes, the quality of life, and symbols of the identity of the person. As we face the problem of living in a probably smaller, different space, the significance of the move is emotionally greater, for the movement often represents the loss of a part of our living that was cherished. It is a goodbye to a significant part of our younger life and a recognition of aging.

The loss of the familiar space of home and neighborhood also unsettles our feelings. Our feelings become colored by anxiousness and fearful anticipations, as well as by sadness. The move will bring the necessity of adjusting to a new place and neighborhood, of creating an inner map of a new neighborhood—to know where we are and how to get there. We will have to undo the automatic reactions and feelings of the old spaces, changing habits as we become accustomed to the new situation. Disorientation and confusion may reign until the new living environment becomes familiar, even automatic.

I remember the day I drove the two hundred miles to my new home. I was about seventy years old and was leaving a home in which I had lived for thirty years. Driving alone in my car, I was not aware of time or even the places through which I traveled. I was like a robot—just traveling. Movements in driving were automatic. Not even the sadness and loss were there; it was just something I had to do. For several months in the new house, I was confused about directions—east, west, and so on. Of course, this was Santa Barbara, where directions really do not make sense. One day I recognized that when the sun rose, it shone in my bedroom window. When I awoke each day, I was facing east. Now I had an internal map and could figure out the basic directions of the house, stores, and so on.

Moving is an emotionally ladened event. Often, we move to a smaller place, as to a senior citizen residence. Familiar sights and sounds are lost. The sense of privacy and intimacy will change. The neighborhood changes.

More importantly, moving means giving up many possessions—such as furniture, clothing, kitchen supplies, and tools. The decisions about downsizing, about what to take, what to give to the children, to give away, or to throw away may bring tears with each loss. Oh, certainly there are things we never liked, things we have not used for years, and things we no longer need. There is some relief at not having responsibility for so many things. Some things we keep out of necessity or from emotional value. The sense of loss prevails; it is a blue time.

In recent years, fires or storms have destroyed many homes. As we leave, through necessity or choice, it is important to keep those things of symbolic importance—both business-wise and emotionally important. Pictures of the family are important; pictures of the past cannot be replaced. They keep us in touch with important episodes in life, with who we are, with who we were, with memories that formed our character. When pictures are lost, the memories may not be as clear or vivid. We are left with an unclear picture of ourselves.

Moving is stress loaded. We often move more than once as we age and require more help for each step. For instance, my mother moved from her home to a sister's family home, to a senior citizen's apartment, and then to a nursing home—all within ten years. This is not that unusual. As we age, we have fewer personal strengths to manage stress. We have less energy, limitations of physical strength and endurance, and less control over events. At a time in life when strangeness is most challenging, we are expected to cope with the most changes.

And yet we do. It helps if the change can be accepted with resilience, readiness, and a smile in the heart. The emotional challenge is to find inner freedom from objects and places—to let go. I look around and know that even though I like my home, it is not me. It might, in some way, represent who I was and am. But the freedom from objects and places brings freedom—a glimpse into who I authentically am. It is a freedom that brings a balance to the inner and outer life; it is me/us—in that new environment.

Mourning losses. Losses bring mourning. The loss of home and/or significant things brings the sadness of grief. For us, the lost home and possessions add to the mourning that aging brings. Sometimes there is also a relief; that period of life is now in the past.

We must honor our feelings and give them expression—to let ourselves go forward on the next path of life.

Chapter 12

Resolving Those Problems
Coping and Control

Age comes. Sometimes it surprises us with its onset, as through a trauma, a stroke, or a heart attack. Other times it creeps upon us in a slower way, gradually depriving us of health or vigor. Through all this, we want, even need, to retain our independence, so that we have some control and a choice about what happens to us and how we are treated.

Parents understand that from about two years of age, most children will assert their will with a resounding "No" when resisting a command. When my niece Lynda was six years of age, her older sister was telling her what to do. Lynda proudly stated, "I don't want you to tell me what to do anymore. I can think for myself."

The need to be the master of our fate grows in our early years, takes flight in adolescence, and remains with us. It does not always work. There are times when we must bow to circumstances, situations, or others. Aging brings about new conditions that affect self-sufficiency.

The desire to be independent; to have our choices honored, and to be in control of our own life lies deep within us. Facing the emotional challenges of growing older, we find that feelings become more intense when events are out of our control and when others seem to take over our lives.

Keeping the Spirit of Independence

We want to maintain an independent lifestyle if possible. Yet as we face the future, independence may not be realistic. The emotional challenges that are anticipated in coping with the loss of independence include accepting the loss of independence as health limitations increase, accepting reliance on others as we lose some independence, and, all the while, maintaining an inner sense of integrity. These challenges are, of course, intertwined. How will we emotionally react to each loss of autonomy as our health problems increase and control over the environment around us decreases?

We strive to keep that spirit of freedom that seems so necessary for our emotional health. *Primary control* is the ability to be in charge of ourselves in environmental circumstances. We can do things for ourselves, take care of our needs and wishes. It is a control that we use in making direct changes in our daily activities. We schedule physical activities. For instance, when the grass is too high, we mow it; when we are hungry, we prepare our food; if we want to go to the store, we get in our car and drive ourselves there; or if we don't like the movie, we leave. We change the environment. We arrange social meetings: yes, I will be at the meeting; no, I won't see that movie. We oversee our lives.

Primary control fades away with aging. When we cannot change or control our environment as we did, we turn to other ways of coping. We turn to indirect methods—*secondary control*. Secondary control is keeping our autonomy by adjusting our personal preferences to situational constraints. This involves control over us, our reactions, and our feelings. Throughout our lives, from childhood on, we master a variety of reactions to difficult situations. One way is to fit into the environment—that is, *changing our attitude and feelings* to respond more positively and pleasantly to whatever is happening. We stay in control by changing our thoughts and especially our feelings to fit more easily into the situation. For instance, in our work-a-day, most of us have had to accept changes brought on by the organization; we learn to make the best of it. Sometimes, it will just take one thought: *I can do that* or *It is not so bad.* Or we can make a conscious effort to change our feelings, as in *I do not have to feel this way.* In this case, we look for something that modifies our reaction—such as *Maybe it won't be so bad. At least if I smile, say thank you, accept what it is, or show gratitude, I will feel better.*

Another kind of secondary control is *accepting the situation*. For instance, if a son or daughter marries a person we don't really like, we accept her/him—and may learn to love him or her. If we find ourselves in the hospital, an optimal reaction is to feel that we are there for our own health—to accept it in good faith and with a hopeful attitude. By this, we simply accommodate ourselves to whatever is.

Another way we accept a difficult situation is through feeling that we had something to do with the situation, as *assuming responsibility* for the event or problem. We somehow caused it or could have avoided it. For instance, "If I had never" or "It was just my good/bad luck." That feeling helps us accept the situation and deal more positively with the anxiety, disappointment, or other feelings that arise.

Some people cope through developing a positive or negative *identification* with another, a more powerful force or person, such as "It is God's will" or "Someone made me do it." These convictions provide some relief, provide a sense that someone is in control, and help us mold ourselves to the situation; it makes us feel better, rather than only as helpless victims.

The wealthy dowager exerts secondary control by giving *orders to others* to carry out her wishes. Most of us do not have that control available! And even then, it may not always work.

There are *passive means* of secondary control; we can choose to avoid a situation that may arouse distressful feelings. We can avoid situations or people who provoke uncomfortable feelings. However, when a situation arises that we cannot change because of illness, some people are so unhappy and desperate that they passively avoid recognition of the situation. I am thinking of the ill person who is helpless, perhaps depressed; he or she turns their face to the wall, unwilling to respond to the love or caring offered them.

Another passive means of control that is often used is meditation and prayer. There is much research that demonstrates the power to alter one's feelings and attitude through both. Essentially, these methods involve taking time to reflect on behaviors, thoughts, and the situation to arrive at an accommodation that provides some inner calm and peacefulness.

We develop these secondary control measures to help us through difficult situations over our lifetime. They are almost automatic now in age and serve us well. To summarize, we exert secondary control when we adjust our feelings to accept a situation and when we accommodate to the circumstances as they are.

Support from others may become necessary. This social support itself can enhance feelings of self-control because our sense of self-worth is directly an outcome of having others who care near us. It makes us feel safe and loved. To the contrary, when help from others is intrusive, it may be experienced negatively and reduce self-esteem. It may result in an unnecessary dependency that belittles the capability of exercising our own judgments.[xxiv] It is important both to accept help and to keep a sense of self-worth throughout.

The challenge awaits us as we age—the challenge of maintaining the ability to make choices about our life, our feelings, and our living conditions; the challenge to accept and feel good within ourselves. We want to stay in charge—as much as possible.

When Does Dependency Start?

Dependency is feared and hated. Submitting to the fear makes it more formidable and changes it to anxiousness. Acknowledging the fear makes it more tolerable, and resolvable.

I have a friend Rita, a very intelligent and capable woman of seventy-five years of age. She made an appointment for a series of treatments with her medical doctor. She told her son about the schedule. Hearing this, he exploded, "Why do you do that? Why do you make appointments without checking with me first?" His reaction surprised her; she knew he was a busy, professional man. She had not relied upon him to take her to the appointments. Once, after cataract surgery, she had needed his help to drive her home, but she was, after all, still comfortable driving to these appointments.

She was nonplussed and could not respond. Yes, he was a caring son, and she loved that. Yet did she have to give up this control of events in her life—already?

Her dilemma was a typical one for an aging parent with caring children. Yes, she had been ill and needed help. Was she now to give up control of all her activities and check everything with her son? Were there alternative ways she could cope with this problem? When do we, as aging persons, accept the control and care of others? How can we cope as we become aware of the need for additional help?

In the end, she chose an alternative means, using friends to help her. But the dilemma remained. He is a loving, caring son. She does not want to offend him. How much control of her life should she, at this point, give up? How much independence must she forego? This friend is at a borderline stage; she is ill. She is keeping her independence as long as possible. She is maintaining her self-efficacy, although she is aware that future support from her son may be necessary. She is coping with her problems on her own.

Solving Problems

This choice of asking for help from friends illustrates that given the opportunity, people make selections from possible resolutions for a problem that will provide them the greatest good. The problem-solving method that she applied is called the *selection-optimization-compensation*.[xxv] The following is one example of the SOC method of problem-solving.

Louise was a seventy-four-year-old widow. Her husband had died ten years earlier. She called herself an independent woman, having retired from an active professional life. She lived in a home that she and her husband had built, was very comfortable there, and intended to stay there. Her plans changed, for she had a minor stroke that affected her walking, and she discovered that she suffered from macular degeneration. Soon enough, she would not be able to see well. She decided to sell her home and move into a senior citizen residence community, where she thought she would feel safer and have help when necessary.

Her first step was to search for residences that would fit her needs—personally and financially. She found five communities in her surroundings from which she would *select* one. She summarized the communities as follows:

- Community A: preferred, more elite, good food, no advanced care such as assisted living, many activities, financially midpriced, pleasant staff.
- Community B: next nicest, food OK, most expensive, three levels of care (independent, assisted living, hospital), some activities, difficult to walk around outside.
- Community C: good external environment, food good, assisted living provided, no nursing home, not many activities, least expensive, staff OK.

- Communities D and E: Both ruled out immediately. Food and care not as adequate, assisted living not provided.

After getting all the information that she could, Louise had to *make a selection*. This is seldom easy, for there are benefits and disadvantages to each. She liked each but for different reasons. If she chose A, she would have to move to another residential setting if the need came for assisted living. That would mean additional planning now for a future move to assisted living. If she chose B, it would be more difficult financially. If she chose C, there might be more difficulty meeting people, activities were limited, and no hospice was provided.

After making her selection, Louise would have to *optimize* the setting to fit her needs. That is, she would have to plan for activities that did not involve vision, such as ease of getting around in the building, the availability of musical programs and other ways that she could enrich the environment for herself.

She selected community B because of the levels of care provided; it was a pleasant environment, *but* she would have to find a way to get around the community more easily. So she decided to use her walker, or if this was not sufficient, to have a motorized scooter to enable her to move about easily in the community. In this way, she was *compensating* for a difficulty she would encounter in community B.

When a problem comes or an important decision must be made—such as Rita's or Louise's—we, as the individuals involved, can first think about and investigate all the possible ways of solving it. Our expectations for living will be readjusted and reevaluated to fit our capabilities and desires. The choices can be made more easily before the necessity arises; after the necessity becomes a reality, it is often more difficult.

Optimization means that consideration of the health conditions is granted the highest priority—such as physical capacities. Then what kind of environment do we desire? For instance, what kind of physical care, rehabilitation programs, recreation programs, and social programs are needed? Personal preferences may be a deciding factor. What does the person especially want—a library, an active social program, or a view of the outside world?

Optimization, to a large extent, depends on stimulating and enhancing environmental difficulties. The question here is, how can we improve the adjustment to the new situation? Baltes reports that "the elderly often live in a world of deprivation, of 'under demand' rather than 'over demand.' For optimization to occur, the elderly must have access to an 'enriched,' perhaps slightly over-demanding environment."[xxvi]

Compensation is aimed at providing alternate means to manage any difficulties the selection may bring. Seldom is there a perfect answer for all problems. Compensation may involve consideration of some physical problems, such as the necessity of wearing a hearing aid. It may require learning new skills—such as adapting to the use of technological processes or learning how to use Skype to have easy communication with others. Or compensation may even require help from others, such as a companion. It is a process of responding to what is missing before it is missed, if possible.

These three are essential processes in any problem-solving process: What is necessary? What is needed in the environment? What are your personal preferences? We then select a choice from among the options.

What is remarkable (or not) is that when presented with difficult problems, it has been shown that we, as senior citizens, *adjust better when we have made the choice*! Of course, discussions with family members or counselors are taken into consideration. The choice, however, should be ours.

Rita selected that, instead of yielding to her son's demands, she would take advantage of the services offered by public transportation or, at times, ask a friend for help. With her choice, she kept control, albeit secondary control, over her activities and daily schedule. She has managed this first stage of coping with some loss of independence quite successfully. It also brought fear and anxiousness with the awareness of possible future dependency.

When we experience these first, although minor, infringements on the inability to maintain our self-efficiency, it is the best time to share our feelings or anxieties about growing older with our spouse and/or family. That sharing is a necessary first step. We need to take the opportunity to express concern and frustration at not having the vigor or strength that once was there. Now is the time to admit uncertainty about what lies ahead. It is a critical time to talk—before anything dire happens. We need to express our wishes; we need to let our feelings about life, illness, and/or death be known. It is the time to plan, make choices, and express choices.

The very idea of feeling it necessary to get permission for daily activities is intrusive, even when help comes from concern and caring. Yet as we age, a time may come when the way we perceive ourselves does not match with the way that others, such as our as children, experience us. Then we arrived at the next stage.

A Growing Awareness

When age creeps up on us, the aches and pains, the unaccustomed tiredness, it forces us to accept help, even for activities we enjoy. I have a friend who, after retirement, loved being outside, working with the flowers, mowing the lawn. An old shoulder injury began to hurt. He gradually realized he needed help with mowing the lawn and trimming the bushes. He would say, "Certainly I can still do it. It is just nice to have help." His sense of control remained, yet he was beginning to depend on others for help. He was unable to perform everyday tasks comfortably, so he sought help from others.

At this point, we develop increasing awareness of physical vulnerabilities as health problems arise. There may be difficulties with vision, hearing, balance, muscle or joint aches, tiredness, memory, or internal physical problems. For those of us who have felt in control of our lives and have made our own choices, either alone or with a partner, the initial reactions to vulnerability are many.

First, we may deny that we are becoming less capable, weaker, and vulnerable. There is dismay that, no matter how well we have treated ourselves, we are getting older. There may be anger for these uninvited health intrusions into our life. A sense of shame about a disability may cause a withdrawal from social engagements. Withdrawal is an attempt to forestall a future need for support from children or others. Whatever the initial reaction, it sets off a mixture of feelings: we are getting older. An underlying sadness can pervade; life is approaching its ending.

One friend, Fran, the mother of six children, has been widowed for three years. Recently, Fran received a preliminary diagnosis of parkinsonism. She still felt good and was very active with friends. One day, after doing several errands, she went out for dinner and an evening concert. While she was out, her oldest daughter, living four hundred miles away, had tried to telephone her mother all day, to no avail. Not being able to contact her mother in the evening, she called a brother, another sister, and then Fran's neighbor. The neighbor checked Fran's home; there were no lights. The brother, who lived ninety miles away, also concerned, drove at midnight to

Fran's home. Fran arrived home five minutes after the son drove in. The neighbor was also there. You know the rest.

They had a good laugh. Fran was at first pleased to know that her children cared so much for her. Then questions arose, how much freedom did she retain to go about her life, enjoying her spontaneity? How could she avoid this in the next instance? How much control should she give up? To whom will she report—and how often? This was just the beginning for Fran. Soon would begin a stronger reliance upon others for support.

At this stage, most of us cope well with the sense that our loss of control and of independence is coming. It is time to prepare for future safety precautions. If we decide for ourselves, we retain some control. We need to prepare a sequence of actions that we would prefer to happen when we need help in the future.

The Shadow of Dependence

Much of our ability to be independent may be lost with the onset of physical illness or disabilities. As health problems arise, we develop a new awareness of our physical vulnerability. The golden age, so-called, has turned the corner.

Ailments now interfere with our ability to cope with everyday activities—driving the car, shopping, preparing food, cleaning the house—all become increasingly difficult. Chronic health problems interfere with our ability to be independent. As time proceeds, caring for the self, as in bathing, dressing, and even cutting toenails, becomes a task rather than the automatic activities they once were. I know one not-so-elderly person, aged sixty-six, who has a podiatrist trim his toenails—his back is stiff enough that he cannot do it for himself. He enjoys that support.

It is difficult to admit the necessity of help or the relief that help might bring. We do not want to burden our children who are in the prime of their lives and busy. The inner strength to ask for help, to let us develop some trust—not submission—uses the second kind of control. That is, expressing our feelings, adjusting our reactions, and letting our wishes be known. To withdraw into loneliness, dissatisfaction, grumpiness, and/or sullen silence spoils the opportunity for pleasant living.

I had one patient, a man of eighty, who lived alone in a senior residence. After his wife died, he skipped breakfast because it took him two to three hours each morning to get washed and dressed. Independent—yes. Too proud (or ashamed) to ask for help? It was available! He had always been stubbornly independent—not wanting help. He refused the care friends would have gladly given. He died alone, in his apartment.

Accepting support is a sign of inner strength, a sign of knowing ourselves.

Autonomy Even with Loss of Physical Independence

Coping during this next phase is difficult and relies upon inner control to keep a spirit of independence. This period of life is marked by the necessity of daily support, whether living alone, with a child's or relative's family, or in an assisted-living residence. Assistance is needed for the necessary activities of eating, bathing, dressing, and so on. We do not really want to be this dependent! Yet it comes to many of us. To cope with this loss of independence brings forth inner strength—that is, our inner autonomy directs our spirit, our feelings, and our reactions to illness.

An autonomous individual acts intentionally, with understanding and choice. Inner autonomy is the freedom of the mind, the feelings, and the spirit. It permits us to cope with whatever comes our way with our feelings that, in turn, direct our actions. Thus, we can act with integrity. Physical dependence is subservient to inner autonomy. With inner control, our sense of self remains alive and alert, no matter the physical limitations.

Autonomy implies an emotional acceptance of and accommodation of external situations while maintaining our integrity. This inner strength becomes the most effective strategy for well-being. Our sense of ourselves as a person is strengthened.

Pain and illness, needful dependency, and even dementia do not destroy our self-awareness. They do not destroy our sense of ourselves. Coping by managing our inner thinking and feelings helps in the acceptance of troublesome, even painful experiences.

Control over external situations brings only a small part of well-being. Wealthy persons with the ability to control their environment and people around them do not necessarily have that inner control that provides a sense of well-being. While these fortunate situations may be desired by all of us, they do not provide a sense of well-being for the person.

Coping and Control

The acknowledgment of limited health, fewer emotional reserves, and declining abilities is a sign of personal strength. To be able to accept some dependency while retaining areas of independence and self-sufficiency leads to a better quality of life and a more successful, contented aging. Primary control over our situation becomes increasingly difficult. The effective use of secondary controls keeps our sense of self and our spirit alive and well. The depression that we see among older persons is not only a surrender of independence but mostly a surrender of autonomy. It is giving up a sense of self, a refusal to cope actively in spirit.

Most effective coping and control involves the use of *selection, optimization, and compensation* for solving problems. In brief, we investigate the possibilities—both emotionally and physically. Then we select from among the choices open to us. We make the optimal choice for ourselves. Since no choice is perfect, we then consider how to compensate for any lack. Most important is to anticipate your emotional reaction in preparation for the change.

Defining one's niche and feeling whole about one's life brings necessary changes and adaptations in old age. The emotional tasks require a balance between dependency, interdependency, and autonomy.

It is important we guide ourselves along our chosen path through these final steps of living as much as possible. We accept our weaknesses; we know our strengths. Then we find new strengths—strengths of our spirit—that we can share with others.

Chapter 13

Aging Wisely

The end of time for the book has come. Time has been gracious to me, for it has taken more than a year to arrive at this point. I do not know, we do not know, what time has yet in store for me or for you. I appreciate each moment that time has allotted me. I hope time will be gracious to you.

I do not quite know how to end this book.

This is a very personal book. I have built into it many of my personal feelings and experiences as well as the professional knowledge that has been with me these many years. Reaching the end of the book brings an end to the two years of writing. These years have been intense, giving me a purpose—that after leaving my clinical practice, I could still hope to help people through those rough spots of life.

As we age, we realize our style of living has been much influenced by our parents, our early experiences, and the effects of the crises we have met. It is difficult to change our personality or our way of reacting to situations. Yet sometimes it is imperative for our own benefit that we change a habit, an approach to persons or problems, or a way of thinking and feeling about situations. To age wisely.

One dear friend died while I was writing this book. A brilliant, successful professional, she was an unusually honest person. She would speak her convictions even when it went against the tenor or grain of those present. She had a brusque, pragmatic manner and was devoted to helping others while finding it difficult to accept care for herself.

In the last month in the hospital, her brusque, demanding manner made it difficult for her to get the immediate care that she wanted. Because of her brusqueness, nurses and assistants sometimes delayed entering her room. And while she waited, her distress grew—with her needfulness and anger. A sad picture to witness, for they waited too long the last time.

To be able to express *gratitude* is of utmost importance, even in the direst of circumstances. Resilience, the ability to adapt to difficult situations, becomes a necessity. Having a sense of gratitude for the smallest of favors done for us seems a gift, yet it is one we can all possess—even or especially when younger—for then it can become a natural inclination to express appreciation of others' efforts. We can develop gratitude at any age. At first, it may be with much effort and lack a good feeling. But as we see the smile and thank you that gratitude brings, it becomes easier and resounds in our souls.

It is never too early to practice those qualities that at least partly assure a sense of well-being in our older years. Conscientiousness, the master trait for living well, applies to all ages. The other traits then seem to fall into order—resilience, coping with difficult situations, attacking fears, managing lonely times; all follow for our benefit.

Love, that awesome connection with others, is wonderful to keep, even when it appears none is available. Love is and makes us tender and kinder to all. A pleasant attitude and optimism help locate the diamond in the darkest times.

Conscientiousness is to accept the gift of life with a spirit of grace. It means to nurture the body, mind, and spirit. It is to exercise integrity and convictions, to be responsible for our works, to be dependable for others, and to give honor to all. It is the spirit of well-being, of gratitude for life itself.

We live life enfolded by the effects of time—by the experiences we had and have, by the accomplishments we shared, by the changes in our physical being, and mostly by the emotional refinements that have led us to love—love for life and love of all around us.

Élan vital and eagerness is a zest and eagerness for life. It embraces the liveliness of spirit and of vitality. Keeping an eagerness for life and retaining pleasure in life is a secret to aging well. To smile through the pain, to greet each day with anticipation, to applaud the success of others, to enjoy the race when unable to walk, to accept one's limitations with contentment, and to have joy as our spirit—these provide élan vital for us.

I wish I had words of wisdom to close the book. Much has been written about old age and the end of life. There is one poem I like:

> The life of man is like a summer's leaf
> Yet few who hear these words take them to heart ...
> You few who understand, know when death is near
> The food you give to your soul must be supreme.
> (Homer)

The time has come to honor the end of the book. I have learned so much about emotional life during these older years. Time has given me new friends who are dear to me. While I do not share a long time in years with them, I value their friendship. I love them. I love each hour with them. Thank you, friends. And thank you, dear reader.

ENDNOTES

Notes to Chapter 3

i   as reported by the Menopause Health Center (2013), "The Emotional Roller Coaster of Menopause," http://www.webmd.com/menopause/emotional-roller-coaster?print=true.

ii   A. Novak, M. Brod, and J. Elbers, "Andropause and Quality of life: Findings from Patient Focus Groups and Clinical Experts," *Maturitas* (2002). NVOrganon: The Netherlands. Contact a.novak@organon.com.

iii   In the report "Hormones and Men" by Dr. Erika (2013), http://drerika.com/content/hormones-men.

iv   From *Death in Venice* by Thomas Mann (New York: Vintage Books, 1930).

v   From *Roots: The Saga of an America Family* by Alex Haley (New York: Barnes and Noble, 2007).

vi   From Big Apple Corner (2013), http://www.barrypopik.com/index.php/new_york_city/entry/when_a_man_retires

vii   Chronic Disease: NCOA, National Council on Aging. http://www.ncoa.org/improve-health/center-for-healthy-aging/chronic-disease/?

viii   Keller, Brenda K, Morton, Joy L. Thomas, Vince S., Potter, Jane F. "The effect of visual and hearing impairments on functional status." *Journal of the American Geriatrics Society*, Vol. 47(11), Nov 1999, 1319–1325.

ix   From "Trends in Health and Aging: Causes of death among older persons in the United States." (2010) By Yelena Gorena, Hoyert, Donna, Lentzner, Harold, and Goordin, Marjorie. Center for Disease Control and Prevention. Center for Health Statistics. http://www.cdc.gov/nchs/agingact.htm.

Notes to Chapter 6

x   From "Older Person's Health" (2010) Center for Disease Control and Prevention. National Institutes of Health. US Department of Health.

xi   Ibid.

xii   Cromie, William J. (2006) "The longer you live, the longer you can expect to live?" (2006), Harvard University Gazette. July 1, 2006.

xiii   Lundman, B., et al., ((2012) "Inner strength in relation to functional status, disease, living arrangements and social relationships among people aged 85 years and older." 2012) Geriatric Nursing, 33,3, pp. 167–176

xiv   Kelley, Maryellen and Cumes, David Michael. (2012) *Messages from the Ancestors. Wisdom for the Way.* Contact: Barbara Gaughen Muller, Literary Agent. Barbara@rain.org

xv   "Anxiety in older adults" (2013). http://www.solutionsforseniorhealth.com/cgi-bin/gt/tpl.h,content=2534

xvi   Senior Health (2012). "Built with You in Mind". http://nihseniorhealth.gov/falls/aboutfalls/01.html

xvii   Perissinotto, Carla M. Cenzer, Irenee and Covinsky, Kennetth. (2012). "Loneliness in Older Persons. A Predictor of Functional Decline and Death." JAMA .Internal Medicine. http://archinte.jamanetwork.com/article.aspx?articleid=1188033.

xviii   Wray, Herbert (2007/2008) "The Aging of Loneliness" http://www.psychologicalscience.org/onlyhuman/2007/2008/aging-of-loneliness.cfm.

xix   From "Aging and Loneliness. Downhill Quickly" (2007) by Louise C. Hawkley, and John T. Cacioppo. Association for Psychological Science, Vol. 16, No. 4.

Notes to Chapter 11

xx   from "A Brief Overview of Adult Attachment Theory and Research" by R.Chris Fraley. (2013). http://internal.psychology.illinois.edu/refraaley/attachment.htm

xxi   Whitbourne, Susan Kraus. (2012). "How to remain productive and healthy into your later years: Bad.Mad.Love" Several studies on the attachment patterns of adults present these results. For more information, see Susan Krauss Whitbourne (2012) From "How to remain productive and healthy into your later years: Bad. Mad. Love." . http://www.psychologytoday.com/blog/fulfillment-at-any-age/201209/bad-mad-love.

xxii   Kaplan, Debra. (2012). "Sex, Love and Attachment" http://

wwwdebrakaplancounseling.com/articles/806
xxiii Maryelen Kelley and David Cumes, MD (2012) From *Messages from the Ancestors. Wisdom for the Way.*

Notes to Chapter 8

xxiv Baltes, Margaret M. (1996) *The Many Faces of Dependency in Old Age.* New York: Cambridge University Press, p. 106ff.
xxv Ibid., pp. 146–150

REFERENCES

Baltes, Margaret M. *The Many Faces of Dependency in Old Age*. Cambridge CB2 1RP: Cambridge University Press, 1996.

Carstensen, Laura L., Derek M. Isaacowitz, and Susan T. Charles. "Taking Time Seriously. A Theory of Socioemotional Selectivity." *American Psychologist* 54, no. 3 (March 1999): 165–181.

Crist, Grace, and Sadhna Diwan. "Chronic Diseases and Aging." Council on Social Work Education. 2010. www:http//csue.org/File.aspx?id-25462.

Daatland, Svein Olav. "The Quality of Life and Aging" in *The Cambridge Handbook of Age and Ageing*, edited by Malcolm L. Johnson. New York: Cambridge University Press, 2005, pp. 372–377.

Dittmann-Kohl, Freya. "Self and Identity" in *Age and Ageing*, edited by Malcolm L. Johnson. Cambridge: Cambridge University Press, 2005, p. 275ff.

Friedman, Howard. "Surprising Discoveries for Health and Long Life." *Landmark Eight Decade Study*. Hudson Street Press, March 2011.

Friedman, Howard S., and Leslie R. Martin. *The Longevity Project. Surprising Discoveries for Health and Long Life from the Landmark Eight-Decade Study*. New York: Hudson Street Press, 2011.

Johnson, Malcolm L., ed. *The Cambridge Handbook of Age and Ageing*. New York: The Cambridge University Press, 2005.

Lockenhoff, Corinna E. and Laura L. Carstensen. "Socioemotional Selectivity Theory, Aging, and Health: The Increasingly Delicate Balance between Regulating Emotions and Making Tough Choices." *Journal of Personality* 72 (December 2004): 6.

Keller-Cohen, Katherine Fiori, Amanda Teller, and Deborah Bybee.

"Social relations, Language and cognition in the 'oldest-old,'" *Ageing and Society*. New York: Cambridge University Press, 2006, 26, 585–605.

Magai, Carol, "Emotions over the Life Span" in James Birren and Warren Schaie. *Handbook of the Psychology of Aging*. 5th Edition. San Diego: Academic Press, 2001.

Moraitou, Despina and Anastasia Efklides. "Affect and Emotions" in *Geropsychology. European Perspectives for an Aging World*. Cambridge, Massachusetts: Hogrefe & Huber Publishers, 2007, pp. 83–102.

National Institute on Aging. Survey Research Center at the University of Michigan. http://www.hrsonline.isr.umich.edu.

Ong, D. "How Positive Emotion Protects Against Poor Health in Later Life" as reported by Ken Pope, Friday, Dec. 17, 2010. At ken@kenpope.com.

Phillips, Edward M., and Donald A. Davidoff. "Normal and Successful Aging: What Happens to Function as We Age" in *Primary Psychiatry* (2007). http://www.primarypsychiatry.com/aspx/article_pf.aspx?articleid=736(1 of 6)8/1/2007.

Selye, Hans. "A Syndrome Produced by Diverse Nocuous Agents." *Neuropsychiatry Classics* 10, no. 2 (spring 1998): 230.

Smith, Deborah B., and Phyllis Moen. "Retirement Satisfaction for Retirees and Their Spouses. Do Gender and the Retirement Decision-Making Process Matter?" *Journal of Family Issues* 25, no. 2 (March 2004): 262–285.

Smith, Dr. habil. Jacqui. "The Fourth Age: A Period of Psychological Mortality?" Max Planck Institute for Human Development, Berlin and Research Group of Psychological Gerontology, Department of Psychiatry, Medial School, Free University, Berlin, 2000, p. 6.

Spector, Tim. "Ageing linked to Social Status." (2010) http://www.news.bbc.co.uk/zh.health/5188742.stm.

Urry, Heather, and James Gross. 2010. "Emotional Regulation in Older Age." http://cdps.sagepub.com

Whitbourne, Susan Krauss, and Sherry L. Willis, eds. "Contemporary Perspectives on Midlife" in *The Baby Boomers Grow up*. Mahwah, New Jersey: Lawrence Erlbaum Associates, Publishers, 2006, pp.164–184.

Zoon, Leonard, Yuri Jang, Sandra G. Reynolds, and Erick McCarthy. "Profiles of the Oldest Old" in *The Cambridge Handbook of Age and Ageing*, edited by Malcolm L. Johnson. New York: Cambridge University Press, 2005, p. 349.